How to Make Money in the Flea Market

How to Make Money in the Flea Market

Joan Bursten
and
Louanne Norris

A Sunrise Book

E. P. Dutton • New York

Library of Congress Cataloging in Publication Data
Bursten, Joan.
How to make money in the flea market.
"A Sunrise book."
1. Secondhand trade. I. Norris, Louanne,
1930-   joint author. II. Title.
HF5482.B87   1978   658.8'7   77-14538
ISBN: 0-87690-278-6
Published simultaneously in Canada by Clarke, Irwin
& Company Limited, Toronto and Vancouver
Drawings by Abner Graboff

10 9 8 7 6 5 4 3 2 1

First Edition

DEDICATED TO ALL THE DEALERS, BUYERS,
BROWSERS, AND COLLECTORS WHO CREATE THE FLEA MARKET

Contents

Part II. The Customer

Part I

The Dealer

1

~~~~~~~~~~~~

The Business of Choice

We didn't choose the flea market business; it chose us. Four years ago on a Friday evening we stood on the crowded floor of a small indoor flea market in New York's Greenwich Village, carrying attaché cases crammed with samples of hand-made bead necklaces. The place vibrated with action. We watched as spirited, energetic buyers handled the old and new merchandise, and we saw money passing from hand to hand.

Mr. Hong, the market owner, offered us a table: $10 for two days, Saturday and Sunday.

"Why not?"

Why not, indeed. If the boutiques that bought our necklaces could sell them, so could we.

Did we have enough necklaces to fill a table? Yes, we did. All those late nights of stringing beads were finally going to pay off.

"If we sell out the first day, we can whip up some more."

"Saturday night?"

"Sure. I can feel those dollars dancing in our pockets and see those necklaces dancing out of the flea market."

Saturday morning, bright and early, we covered our table with three yards of deep red velvet and laid out dozens of brightly colored necklaces. They glittered blue, green, yellow, orange. Who could resist them?

But there they stayed, and stayed and stayed. . . . All those lovely people just glanced at them and kept right on walking.

"OK, Louanne, that's it. I'm going to walk the aisles and find out what's happening here."

Twenty minutes later Joan was back at our table, excited at what she'd discovered. "Everyone is buying old things, the way they do at a rummage sale. Tomorrow we're filling our table with the same kind of junk. Go take a look."

That night we dug deep into closets, trunks, and cartons packed years ago. We came up with dishes from broken sets, Mickey and Minnie Mouse glasses, a souvenir medallion, old silk scarves, costume jewelry from our teenage years, a Pinocchio with a broken arm, two lace tablecloths, you name it. We had more than enough to fill a tabletop.

We staggered into the flea market on Sunday morning with our loaded cartons. We dumped the contents on the table helter-skelter. The prices were whatever popped into our heads —$1, $2, $3. The top was $5. Customers flocked to our table. Fingers and hands were all over the place. And a clamor of voices:

"Can you do any better than $2?"

"Sure, make it $1.50."

"Would you take $3 for the dishes?"

We were both talking and taking in money right and left.

Our sales came to $140, and none of it had cost us a penny. We had had fun and we had made money. We were hooked!

During the week we ransacked again, but this time slowly and more carefully. We looked at everything differently. Old cigarette cases and compacts that we hadn't used for years— they were silver and enamel, and someone would want them. And someone did. That waffle iron could go and other kitchen implements. A lot of people who bought our things the first Sunday came back to us the next week. A few became steady customers until the day a year later when we finally left Mr. Hong's Flea Market for a more prestigious one with a larger public.

Where to Sell? Your Choice

Flea markets are where you find them, and these days they seem to be all over the place: large cities, suburbs, small towns, and farm country. There are the permanent, usually large and famous markets that you will surely want to visit at least once if you haven't already been there. We are still fascinated by the Englishtown Flea Market in New Jersey and we can't stay away. On a trip to California Joan visited the monthly Rose Bowl Flea Market in Pasadena, where thousands of dealers do business buying and selling. Louanne visited the North Carolina Super-Flea and found hundleds of deaers there, drawn from all over the state and out of state as well.

But when it comes to your own business, it's probably best to begin at a small local market. Learn the ropes before you climb to the top of the trapeze. Read your local papers, eye the lamppost and bulletin boards, ask friends, even antique dealers. Then visit the flea markets that sound right to you and pick the one that is most appealing because:

> It is nearest your home or easy to get to.
> It has a good reputation.
> It is crowded with customers.

What to Sell? Your Choice, Too

The simplest way to begin is to sell your own belongings. Walk around your home and look at everything with a fresh eye. Do you need it? Do you want it? Perhaps you'd love to be rid of it, once and for all. There is, indeed, a buyer for everything. Whatever you choose to sell, there is someone out there who will choose to buy it—at the right price. Think dollars and cents. How much would you pay for it if you really wanted to own it?

You need volume sales to make money. The more things you bring, the more things you'll sell. Open drawers and closet doors. Poke into attics and cellars. If you're unsure about an item, bring it anyway. The higher the jumble on your table, the more people you'll attract, every last one of them a potential buyer with money in his pockets.

Not enough? Ask your relatives, your neighbors, your friends. Our friend Allison, mother of three college students, had carefully kept everything a baby and a small child possibly use or have fun with, and all of it had been used by all three of her children. We asked Allison if she'd like to get rid of it all.

"I'm glad you asked me. Otherwise I would have kept them forever. Maybe some other child can enjoy them. I need the storage space, but I couldn't bear to just throw these things out. You'll be doing me a favor if you take them."

We sold games of the fifties and sixties, comic books, baby books, and old rattles. As well as lovely dresses—the sort a baby wears once or twice and then outgrows—lamps shaped like elephants, a powder jar with Donald Duck dancing around the rim. Bless you, Allison, and all the others who helped us get started.

How Expensive Will It Be?

How much money you need to begin your business is, again, up to you. You may prefer to invest in stock even before you begin to sell. You'll need $50 to $100 to set up, really overload, your first table, with some backup just in case the buyers overwhelm you. (It sometimes happens to beginners.) You can expect to spend several weeks or even months searching and traveling, buying the things that attract you. But, remember that if you put down money for your merchandise, you won't be able to start out as impulsively as we did. If freebies don't sell, well, they haven't cost you anything. You pack them up and sigh. But if what you buy doesn't sell, you're in trouble.

It's a good idea to begin selling as soon as possible. You need market experience and customer feedback. They are the only things that will tell you whether or not you're on the right track.

The only other large expense is your space rent. It can range anywhere from $2 to $50.

No matter how hard you try, you can't spend a great deal of money in the flea market business.

Profits from the Start

Your profits can begin the first day, if not the first hour, you spend at the flea market. Whether they get larger or stay the same is up to you.

Your money making begins the first day, and so does your chance to learn. Keep your eyes open. Don't watch your fellow dealers. Watch their customers—the people who actually buy, not the browsers. What on your table attracts the most attention? Watch everything the way you watch a stage play, a movie screen. You'll find yourself learning and learning fast. Apply what you learn. Search out and buy more of the things your customers buy from you. Learn what they want to pay. That will determine the price you pay for your merchandise. A well-dressed man paid you $14 for a box of brass weights that cost you $6. He paid the additional $8 for the trouble *you* took to search them out, the time *you* spent doing it, the early hour *you* got up on Sunday to get to the flea market in time to be set up for business when he got there, and the hard work *you* invested. You really earn your profit. That's lesson number one.

2

Recycling

Beginnings

If you begin your flea market career as we did—by selling your own things—or if you start from scratch, after a few weeks your cupboards will be bare. Don't panic. There is plenty of secondhand and antique merchandise to be found— most of it interesting, some of it exciting, almost all of it a potential source of profit for you.

At times, making our way gingerly through cellars in old houses, poking through cartons stored in barns and shooing away the birds that nested on them, we've thought of ourselves as ragpickers. If we are, we belong to a very old calling. The ragpickers of medieval Europe, a dirty and raucous lot, sold their goods in one or two specific locations in each city. These were called *flea* markets for good reason, although, thank heaven, that reason no longer holds true.

They could have been called recycling markets, since any

XXX Cookie Co.—Main Street General Store

1890—an anniversary present for Mrs. Smith—xxx cookies

1900—it holds spools of thread

1910—now in the kitchen for coupons

1920—forgotten, on the shelf in the garage

1930—now it holds granddaughter's jewelry

1940—her love letters

1950—given away, goodness knows where

1960—sold to a bride: "I love it for the coffee table!"

1970—bought by a flea market dealer at an apartment sale and resold to a young mother, "for cookies, of course," on the kitchen shelf

1980—it stores puzzle pieces

secondhand item, once again in use, is recycled. That's what the secondhand market, and particularly the flea market, is all about.

In this country flea markets arose naturally out of the weekly farmer's market. Along with his produce, the farmer brought whatever hard goods he no longer had a use for. His wife and children carried to market the crafts they had worked on during the winter months: bits of whittled wood, needlework, handmade toys. In recent years, we've seen a surge of interest in both the secondhand and the handcrafted items. The two seem to complement each other. Truly handmade, lovingly crafted items are hard to resist, and something secondhand—not old enough to be antique but aged enough to be exotic and interesting—has become unique because of the uses it was put to in the past. As with handicrafts, no two items are exactly alike. They've been touched by human hands, over and over, until they've acquired a distinctive patina.

A New Use

"Now what do you call that?" Joan asked the dealer at the next table. We were busy setting up, arranging and rearranging the stock on our tables, getting into the carnival spirit of the town's big yearly street fair. Hundreds of people would soon come strolling by.

"Wish I knew *what* it was used for. Whatever, it's definitely brass and it's got to be worth the 75¢ I'm asking," the other dealer replied.

Joan picked up the small brass disk. It had one-inch spikes sticking straight up, about two dozen of them. "I'll take it," she said impulsively, to Louanne's surprise.

"But what will you say when the customer asks you the same question?"

"I'll give the same answer he gave me. No problem." Joan put a $2 price sticker on it and waited.

Early in the afternoon a young woman picked it up. "I've seen wire frogs and pottery frogs, but never one in brass."

"Could you tell me please what exactly these 'frogs' were used for?" Joan asked.

"Oh, you put the frog in a vase and press each flower stem into the spikes for a formal arrangement. But I need it for another use," our customer confided. "My ring collection is getting too big to jumble up in a box. With this I can display two or three rings on a spike, and anyway, I love the look of old brass." Handing Joan the $2, she walked away.

Rediscovering the Original

A few months after we began our flea market business, Joan's husband, Walter, brought home the ugliest lamp we had ever seen. It had a marble base on which stood the bronze figure of a woman draped in large feathers and with a very smug expression on her face. She was topped by a tall silk shade with more feathers on it—obviously custom-made to match the figure. Walter's reasoning? "I couldn't resist its ugliness or its price, $15, and anyway I'm going to take it apart and you can sell each piece separately."

We ended up with one round marble disk with a large indentation—an ashtray, of course. One figure of a lady with feathers that turned out to be a signed bronze. And a rectangular piece of fine old silk with a hand-painted feather design.

On our next market day we sold the ashtray and silk early on, at $8 each. But the bronze just stood there and waited. Finally, one day a man walked up. He looked at the signature on the base of the bronze and his face suddenly lost all expression, as if he were a player in a poker game. We knew what that meant. Luckily we had neglected to put a price sticker on the feathered beauty. Louanne stood up and said confidently, "$100 for a signed, original bronze. That's a really good price."

"You're right," he said, "I'll take it." As we packed it in a supermarket shopping bag, he told us, delighted, "You can't imagine what a marvelous lamp this will make. I've always wanted an original French bronze."

Nostalgia

When a browser stops at your table, picks up an item, turns it slowly in his hand, and you watch as a dreamy smile appears on his face, that's it—nostalgia. That browser will become a buyer. He'll ask if you can get him others like the one he bought. He'll be back week after week. After a while he will think of himself as a collector. "I collect old kitchen scales. Have you any? I bought one from you months ago. If you get any more, call me at this number. I'll come down the next Sunday and buy it—but it has to be old."

This will happen over and over again. If it isn't kitchen scales, it will be something else.

We arrived at Mr. Hong's Flea Market early one Sunday morning and found an electrician standing on our table repairing a ceiling light. He moved to another table, and we began setting up our stock, but we noticed him watching our tabletop out of the corner of his eye and wondered just what had attracted his attention. It was a bar of soap decorated with a Donald Duck design, and it was in mint condition.

"Say, I like that. Never saw one before. How much?" He bought it for $1.

The very next Sunday, he was back, frantic. "My son found that bar of soap you sold me and used it in the shower. Can you get more?"

Luckily we had more. We had bought a box of three bars. And we had found another collector—this time of anything with Donald Duck on it.

Everything that is old and unique has a nostalgia value, and that is what makes it salable. The more unusual it is, the more collectible it is. Nostalgia is the greatest thing ever to happen to the flea market business. Such TV series as "The Waltons" and "Happy Days" trade on nostalgia for their popularity. There is no reason you shouldn't do the same in your business.

Search out and price your merchandise with nostalgia in mind. If it's just an old pretty plate, nostalgia won't apply. But if the plate had a unique and specific use in the past (like a mustache cup), or a name or pattern that evokes the past and gives rise to sentiment, you're in. A flea market stock that relies on nostalgia sells more quickly and at a higher rate of profit.

Any time a browser walks up to your table, picks up an item, holds it aloft and pipes—always in a loud voice—"Why would anyone want to buy this?" you have a foolproof answer.

"Because it reminds them of times past. It's a prime bit of nostalgia."

3

The Portable Shop

How Much Can You Carry?

When would-be dealers ask us, "How much stock do we need to get started?" our answer is always the same: "How many cartons will your car hold?" or "How much can you cram into the trunk of a taxi?"

The answer to that question is all-important. It determines the size of your stock. The question is not how much stock you need, but how much stock you can handle. You need as much as you can carry to market.

Harry is the very first friend we made at the flea market. For the past six years he has been earning his entire living working the same indoor market, in spring and fall, and for variety, the same outdoor Sunday market each summer. In winter he travels and shops for stock. Harry knows exactly what he can pack into his station wagon.

"It is," Harry told us one day, "sixteen large cartons, with two picnic tables, a large round sun-umbrella, and a canvas chair tied on the roof. And I have to be very careful about what I buy. I must turn my merchandise over fast, or I'm not making enough money. If an item doesn't sell in a few weeks, it's just so much wasted carton space. That item is taking up room that could be used for another, more salable one."

We had to agree. Joan added: "A shop owner has no problem. He can buy and buy and just load it into the store, shelves up to the ceiling and shelves in the basement. That's what he's paying a monthly rental for."

"That's just what I mean," Harry continued. We were all standing at the day's end in a near-empty parking lot with our cartons. "We're all paying a day's rent, two day's rent. Everything I sell has to fit into that wagon. If I sell enough items to fill two cartons on Sunday, I can bring two cartons of fresh merchandise the following week."

"It snowballs," Louanne chimed in.

"Someday I'm going to work up to a minibus and then to a good-sized van. That's my long-range goal," Harry summed up.

If you're smart, you'll take advantage of Harry's experience. Have you been buying up old photos for resale? Weed out the uninteresting ones and leave them at home. Take the ones that grab your eye first when you flip through the whole box. They'll sell much more quickly and your customer will appreciate your being selective. He has a lot of everything to look at, to handle, and to make decisions about at the market. Make it as easy for him as you can. Perhaps you'll sell a few more cartons each week.

Pick the Pluses

Children love to play the "cloud game." You lie on the sandy beach or the cool park grass and stare up at the summer sky with its pure white clouds. What does the shape of that cloud remind you of: a lily, a dog, a jet plane, a space rocket? How many different shapes can you find in a cloud? How many different selling points can you find in one old postcard, one 78 record, one pottery teapot? Let's look at them.

For the postcard, customers like:

> Real photos of American towns
> Cards mailed from Cripple Creek, Colorado
> Anything having to do with mining towns
> Photos with horse and buggy
> Cards tinted sepia
> Pictures of real storefronts

For the 78 record, buyers collect:

> Any recording by Billie Holiday
> Benny Goodman records, pre-1940
> Pop records with funny titles
> ("Your Mother's Son-in-Law")
> Jazz of the 1930s

For the teapot, browsers are looking for:

> A small teapot: "I'm on the coffee wagon."
> Anything with dragons
> Dark red pottery to brighten a white kitchen
> Bric-a-brac stamped "Occupied Japan"

All these points of interest we found in one card, one record, one teapot in our stock.

When you buy, buy the pluses. Train your eye to see them. Your stock will appeal to many more people and will sell that much faster. You can't carry everything, so skim the cream. Leave the milk for the next dealer.

Flea markets sometimes specialize in a particular category. One Sunday we found ourselves in a hotel ballroom surrounded by what seemed to be millions of miniatures. An annual event for dollhouse collectors, the show included everything any dollhouse would need to be complete. There

"Got any Artie Shaw 78s?
Or political pinbacks?"

"Any shoehorns today?"

"What's that?"

"Do you have
any die cuts?"

"Tell me about them."

"What's the price of
the figural cookie jar?"

LISTEN TO YOUR CUSTOMERS

we found an impossibly tiny glass cup and saucer with a hand-painted design and gold rims, circa 1910. We bought it at $6. Did we sell it to be used in a dollhouse? Did we sell it to a collector of miniatures? Did we sell it to a glass collector? No, no, and no. We sold it to a middle-aged couple, both of whom squinted at the design, the insignia of a small German resort town. They paid us $14, delighted with their find. They hadn't seen anything with that insignia in the last two years, and that's what they collected.

Go for the New

For dealers at the flea market the question, "What's new?" isn't a casual one. It's an important aspect of the business as a whole.

Every week at Mr. Hong's Flea Market we saw many of the same faces, again and again. At least sixty percent of the browsers came every weekend, all asking that same question: "What's new?" It wasn't hard for us to learn the right answer.

"Oh, we bought a large lot last week at a rummage sale (auction, yard sale, whatever)." That was the answer that stopped the browser like a red traffic light and brought his attention to our stock.

Search for new items. If you've never sold it before or seen any other dealer selling it, that's a plus. You can surprise the jaded taste. No one has seen everything.

Spend some time visiting the decorative arts section of your local museum. If you can, travel to a few of the historical restorations. Williamsburg in Virginia was the first and is probably the best known. Visit the landmark houses in your area. You can get ideas for new items to stock by paying attention to the details, the small artifacts in each room.

Read the popular home magazines. Look carefully at the photos. Take advantage of the ideas the expensive designers are promoting in them.

We like Janet as a personal friend; we admire her as a clever dealer. She spends a lot of time reading and searching out new ideas. Her table always has at least one surprise on it. And that's what keeps her customers coming back, week after week.

Recently she read an article on the fashion page of her local paper. "It really got me excited," she told us. "There were photos of wealthy and famous women at a society gathering. All of them carried little white hankies, lace-trimmed and very Victorian." The article had mentioned a well-known antique-clothes shop where the hankies were available. The prices were devastating. "And there I was with a good stock of handmade white trimmings. I bought old, ripped, stained cotton, old doilies and runners and removed all the lace and crochet that was still in good shape. Here was my chance to sell it big." She had flipped through the Yellow Pages and found a wholesaler who would sell her plain white cotton hankies in lots of six dozen, at a wholesale price. "I trimmed just one of them with the best quality lace I owned and mounted it on a piece of white board as a sample."

"That way you don't spend your time at the sewing machine. Remind us never to. . . ." Louanne added.

But Janet talked on: "The customer buys the hankie and the trim from me, choosing the style of trim from my large stock, and does the sewing herself. She's being creative and I'm making money."

Leave Your Taste at Home

Louanne loves old stuffed toy animals—the smaller, the better. Joan adores very old, blackened muffin tins—the more dents, the more adorable. How about you? Whatever it is, think hard. Do you sell as many as you can find? Do customers ask you to get more? Is anyone collecting them? If you have to answer no, think hard again. Are you trying to sell your own taste? Well, nobody's going to buy it unless it happens to coincide with theirs.

Leave your taste for your own private life, where you can indulge that taste as you please. We can decorate our own homes with all the muffin tins and old stuffed animals we can find. But if you see us carrying them to the flea market, whisper in our ears, as gently as you can: "That's your taste, not ours."

4

The Personal Touch

Shopping Mall vs. Flea Market

We love to visit indoor shopping malls. The newer, the better. All that chrome, brick, and natural wood. Those bright and lovely lights. All that glamor, all that money spent to beautify, to entice your dollar. To be there is like being in a never-never land: airy and clean, everything always new and crisp.

Each seems to have its own style and identity. There's only one thing about it that's anonymous: the people. Who chooses the merchandise, who buys it, who decides on its display, who decides the price you pay? Can you remember the salesgirl who waited on you? Of course you can't. She's been trained to be as impersonal as possible. That way, she can handle more customers in each hour and ring up more sales.

What a contrast to the flea market! Sometimes you wonder if someone isn't running a contest, with the prize going to the drabbest looking flea market to be found. There are never enough lights indoors, and they are never arranged to enhance your merchandise. Outdoors, there's complete lack of protection from the sun and possible rain. No money is ever spent to glamorize the surroundings. They are as anonymous as they can possibly be.

Then what is there about the flea market that is glamorous? What gives each individual market its own style, its own color?

You do. You and all the other dealers who bring the items you choose to sell at the prices you choose to sell them at; who choose the way you arrange them in your spaces, and the coverings on your tables, if you choose to cover them at all. The glamor of the flea market, for its customers, is in the personal touch of the dealer. That dealer—with some help from his friends—buys, prices, displays, cleans, sells, wraps, travels, searches, profits.

Here is a shopping mall where the customer deals directly with people who will talk to him and carry on a dialogue about his collections, his memories, his interests. Here are people who are flexible, willing to talk price, willing to make an effort to find more of what the customer wants to buy, just for him—a personal service. No two market dealers are alike. And it's those very differences between them that make the flea market such a fun place. The browser never knows what to expect from the dealer, both by way of the merchandise he stocks and the manner in which he sells it. The unexpected is the spark behind the success of every flea market.

Since new shopping malls are always opening up, and more and more flea markets are appearing on the scene, it's almost as if the public needs one to balance the other..

In fact, flea markets are being set up in the large promenades of many of the indoor shopping malls. Of course, the lighting in these promenades does nothing to enhance the secondhand merchandise. There are no sparkling glass cases and chrome counters. It's the same old drab, catch-as-catch-can display. And the customers love it. They can continue to buy new things impersonally and efficiently, while indulging their taste for the old and the eccentric, and acquire those things in the old warm, personal style of buying.

Dealers Make a Market

The rent you pay for a space at any flea market covers more than just the number of square feet in that space. You're also buying the style of that market, and it's the other dealers who make that style, whatever it is. You're buying those other dealers' talents and abilities and the customers they attract. Their stock can enhance yours or it can downgrade yours. And, of course, how you handle your business will reflect on them.

Before you decide to join any market, visit it several times. Look at everything. Ask questions. Does it have a good reputation for:

Honest dealing?   Friendly people?
Realistic prices?   A relaxed atmosphere?
Desirable merchandise?   Accessibility?
Reliable dealers?   A large public?

If all these factors are present, then you should also see there the most important element . . .

Money Changing Hands at a Fast Pace

If it is, then that's where you will want to set up your business.

But if the answer is no to any of the above questions, keep on looking. You want to get full value for your rent money.

One day our friend Janet insisted on taking us to visit a large indoor, permanent flea market. Dealers rented small spaces by the month. It seemed a good solution to the "what do we do all winter and during the week" problem.

"You won't believe this place," Janet said. "It's a perfect example of what not to aim for." And she was right. The dealers all seemed nervous and uptight. We could sense a strong animosity among them. It kept getting in our way whenever we tried to look at the merchandise, which is, after all, what the customer is interested in doing.

"Well," exclaimed Janet later, over afternoon coffee, "you know never to go back. No money changed hands there. Still, it's a shame. A lot of the stock was well chosen and displayed, but those dealers turn off the public. Not to mention each other."

"But why do they stay?" we wondered. "They obviously can't be making much money."

"Now you're asking one of those impossible questions that no one can answer. I don't know how many flea markets I've seen that bring up that same question. Some people just love to move in, plunk themselves down, and not move, ever, unless forced to."

The next time you're thinking about moving to a new market, walk in. Look around and listen. Are there good vibes or unpleasant ones? Stay away from that nervous tickle in the air. There are plenty of pleasant, relaxed flea markets out there. Their good vibes will help your business.

Be Yourself

The best advice ever is to be yourself. And it's just as important in the flea market as anywhere else.

One afternoon at an outdoor flea market on an urban parking lot, we made a list of all the unusual bits of clothing we saw some of the dealers wearing:

> A large-brimmed straw farmer's hat
> A fire chief's headgear
> A black top hat
> An organdy garden hat with roses
> A black derby with Indian feathers
> Denim overalls
> An Indian sari
> A silk evening skirt
> A bathing suit over tights

It seemed to be a matter of anything goes, as long as it called attention to the dealer and impressed his image on the customer's mind. If that's where you're at, fine. If not, don't worry. Most dealers don't indulge their fancies when it comes to dress.

What they do indulge are their emotions and their response to the customer. When you work for yourself, you don't have to please anybody else. That's what it means to be your own boss. Of course, the more customers you please, the more your business will increase.

Most of your business transactions at the market will be pleasant and rewarding, but there are always exceptions. If an unpleasant situation arises, remember, you don't have to take it quietly. Be yourself and fight back if that's your response.

Susan and Alex had been in business only a few months when they learned that.

Susan was very proud of a long string of large, heavy, round beads, dark green with thin lines of red. They were bloodstones, old and unusual. Early in the afternoon a man stopped at their table, slowly picked up the beads, and frowned. "What do you call these?" he asked in a loud, rough voice.

"Bloodstones," answered Susan. "They're Victorian."

"They're what?" The man laughed. "You mean they're from the five and dime store, maybe ten years old," he sneered, and then threw the string down on the table. "I'll give you $2 for them."

"Well," Alex said calmly, "they are tagged at $60, so I guess you had better just forget about them."

"I won't forget them. If you sell them for more than the $2 I'm offering you are cheating the customer and I will report you to the manager."

"Look," said Alex, "I'm getting annoyed and soon I'll get angry, so just let the beads alone. I'll even call your bluff; please do complain to the management."

The man walked away muttering. The beads were sold

later that afternoon for $60, to someone who knew their worth.

Remember that a flea market is an open place. Anyone can walk in and sometimes does. All you have to do is ask the offensive browser to leave your table. Say it strongly, and he or she will get the message.

Make It Work for You

To make your business work for you, personally, keep in mind the following tips.

Keep Up a Rapport with Your Customers

No matter how much help you have from family, friends, or partners, wait on as many buyers yourself as you can. Talk to anyone at your table who has something knowledgeable to say about your stock.

Do Your Own Buying

The more time you spend buying for resale, the faster you'll be able to make decisions. Is the price right? Is that item going to upgrade your stock?

Keep Learning

The more you know, the more fun you'll have at the flea market. You'll be gaining confidence in your ability to handle anything and everything.

Stay Flexible

Ride with the taste of your customers. If nobody wants to rummage through antique buttons any more, leave that jar at home. Take the new fad in its place.

Keep Moving Your Shop

Remember, it's portable. Like a snail, you can carry your shop anywhere you please. Keep trying new markets. Revisit the old ones. Taking a summer vacation? Plan an itinerary of flea markets. Try to reach the in-town markets each Sunday, to look about or to buy. Do your vacationing on weekdays.

Never let your interest flag. If you hit a lull, if at any time it all begins to bore you, you'll need drastic remedies. Cut your prices and put a large sign on your table:

EVERYTHING CHEAP!

GOING OUT OF BUSINESS

With the kind of action that sign brings, you're going to find your interest renewed, and you're back in business.

5

How to Buy

Don't Be Stingy

Is it absolutely necessary to spend money to make money? It sure is! The more you spend on merchandise, the higher your potential profits. You can't make money if you're too tight to let go of your hard-earned dollars. Recycle those dollars, and they will earn you more.

Our first flea market experience, selling our own useless trash, resulted in:

Gross	$140.00
Rent	--10.00
	$130.00
Cab fares	−4.50
Net	$125.50

"Wow, can we have a good time with that," Louanne said. "It's found money. Straight out of nowhere."

"You're right," Joan answered. "It's like an unexpected gift."

But as we thought about it, we recognized there were two clear alternatives:

1. We could have a good time spending it all on fun things.
2. We could have a good time buying stock and getting our flea market business on a truly professional basis, really putting our ideas and opinions to the test. Will people buy what we offer, at our price?

That's right, we went for number two. And we still are doing just that. The first thing we learned was that you can't sell what you haven't got.

You must keep looking, no matter where you travel or what it is you are shopping for. Decide how much you want to spend and spend it. Each dollar you earn in the flea market can be turned over again and again, earning more dollars. Your income will increase and so will your business.

Buying in Volume

A large part of your business will be from things that you can retail for under $5. Most casual shoppers want to bring home "something," but an inexpensive something. Is it possible to make money selling items for 50¢ or $1? It sure is, and many a dealer finds himself earning more profit at that price than he does with his higher-priced, harder-to-sell merchandise.

The trick is in buying by the carton, not by the piece.

In the back of an old store Susan found a carton of slogan buttons, each with a long pin at the back, circa 1943, bearing World War II insignia. The shopkeeper wanted $12 for them.

Susan hesitated. "We've never sold buttons before. Does anyone buy World War II?"

"We'll soon find out," Alex laughed. "At $12 a carton I just can't pass it up."

That night they sat on the floor and counted. How many buttons? There were 1,832, all in good condition.

"But how much can we sell them for?"

"Well," said Alex, "at 25¢ apiece, that's 1,832 quarters. And that comes to $458. So allowing for volume discounts to our customers, we can't get less than $400 back for our $12 investment."

"But don't forget, it's going to take time to sell that many buttons."

"At that rate of profit the time factor is well covered."

Alex was right. They sold $14 worth of buttons the first day. After that, it was pure profit. For all we know, Susan and Alex are still selling the World War II buttons and still making a profit on their $12 investment.

One at a Time

You'll buy your better merchandise one at a time. Find what you can, where you can. But most important, buy it at the very lowest price you can talk it down to.

Try to turn even the single pieces you want into volume purchases. Here's one method that will help. If the dealer you're buying from knows you are interested in eight or nine of his things, he'll be willing to work with you on price.

1. Ask the price of each item separately.
2. Add them together:

Oil lamp	$9.00
Celluloid necklace	3.00
Framed print	7.50
China tea set	18.00
Three postcards	1.00
Plastic handbag	4.00
	$42.50

3. Ask (sweetly) if he can let you have them all for $35.
   "Well, $40 would be my bottom line. I'm not making much as it is."

"How about $38? The creamer is missing from the tea set, and I'll have to look around for another to match."

"Oh, all right, take it all for the $38, but it's a steal. It's hard to find this kind of merchandise now."

Never mind his complaints. You saved $4.50 by putting it all together, and there are times when you will do even better. But remember, you want to buy only those things you have a good chance of selling. You can take greater risks with your volume purchases, but be careful with the high-priced things you buy singly.

Cultivating your suppliers is another way to lower the price you pay for each piece in your stock. If a businessman sees that you are coming back again and again to buy and that you are serious about buying, he will give you his lowest price. Keep going back. Even if you find nothing you can sell, or nothing you can afford, eventually he may turn up something you can use. And because you are friendly and have worked up a rapport with him, the price will be right.

Remember that although you are buying right now for next week's or next month's market, you will also be buying six months and a year from now. You will need merchandise then just as you need it now. Making friends with your current sources and even potential ones, no matter how far-fetched they may seem, will help you buy a better grade of merchandise at a lower price.

Never Refuse a Bargain

At a rummage sale we visited last month, there was a very short Victorian necklace, probably for a small child, hanging on a metal rack surrounded by strings of cheap plastic beads. It was made of bits of coral on a gold chain with a rose engraved on the flat clasp, and was tagged at $1. Truly a bargain. Why didn't we buy it? Well, we kept thinking of the small size, and while we hesitated, someone else bought it. Could we have sold it?

1. Antique jewelry is more popular now than ever before.
2. We see so many very slim woman, the size would not have been a problem.
3. Loose pieces of antique coral are salable to our customers who make their own jewelry.
4. The clasp could have been strung on the gold chain as a "nothing" pendant.

We missed that opportunity. Don't you ever hesitate if the price is right.

Think Dollars and Cents

"It's so hard to resist," Harry sighs.

"Resist what," we asked.

"All those rusty old carpentry tools," he answers. "Most of them are too expensive for me. I can't pay the going price and resell at a good enough profit. I just have to pass them by. But I love them all the same. The older and rustier, the better I like them."

"Cheer up," we said, trying to be helpful. "You can always buy yourself the most expensive, rustiest carpentry tool at the country's largest flea market, tie a red ribbon around it, and give yourself a birthday present. You deserve it, if anybody does."

"Right you are," he said with a smile, "and no problems with cost and overhead. Or profit."

Harry is very careful, and so should you be. Try hard never to confuse your own marvelous taste with your profit motive. No matter how much you love it, if you can't make money on it, walk away.

6

Where Does It All Come From?

Original Sources

Have you ever looked at a row of flea market tables, each with its wide variety of merchandise piled high (there's never enough room), and wondered: Where, in heaven's name, does it all come from?

That first flow of manufactured goods in the late nineteenth century was the beginning of it all. For the first time, goods were made with a mass market in mind. For the first time, these goods were advertised and promoted. Companies competed for the same dollar. Premiums were given away—free —in an effort to persuade the customer to buy and buy again. The success of this type of promotion was enormous. And so more attention was paid to these inducements, until they almost matched the level of the made-to-be-sold goods, both in style and quality.

We are talking about a grade of quality almost unknown

in modern manufactured goods. Today's economic realities make such quality impossible. The price of almost anything similar would be out of your reach and ours. If quality is what your customer wants, he has come to the right place. The flea is one of the last marketplaces where he can still buy it.

Our dealer friend Susan has a real love of fine leather. She can't resist a well-made piece. One day she found a large portfolio, made to hold letter paper and envelopes. Eighteen inches wide and twenty-four inches long, it must have sat on the flat top of an enormous desk. J. P. Morgan's, perhaps? Well, we can all daydream. But the portfolio itself was real. Soft, flexible leather with a Persian design embossed on the cover. Inside, it was lined with heavy brown silk. Obviously, it had been well taken care of. Susan paid $2 for it at a rummage sale and priced it at $12. Hoping no one would buy it, she tried to cover it with a pile of books.

"If it's still here in a month, it's yours," promised her partner Alex. "After all, we have to have something on our table to sell."

By ten o'clock that morning it was gone. Its quality and modest price made it irresistible to the buyer, who promised to stop by the next week, just in case Susan and Alex turned up more top-quality leather goods.

"Well," sighed Susan, "at least I know it's gone to a good home. He loves it as much as I do."

"And it looks like we've made a steady customer," said Alex. "All we have to do is get him more of the same."

"Not easy," Susan laughed. "But if anyone can find it, we can."

Will It Keep Coming?

It sure will. The 1920s and 1930s still mean quality and even more—high style, art deco, moderne. Picture Jean Harlow in a heavy white silk gown, leaning on an overstuffed square lounge chair. Watch those films on late-night TV and really look at everything: clothes, furniture, the dozens of small details. They will tell you just what art deco really is, whether it originally came from Tiffany's or Woolworth's. What about right now? What's turned up in the last twenty years that you can sell five years from now? Plenty. Anything having to do with:

The Beatles
Any early rock group that no longer exists
Space travel
The anti-Vietnam War movement
Astrology
The Bicentennial
Queen Elizabeth's Silver Jubilee
Comic characters
Books on photography: recent, but out of print
Short-lived music styles: be-bop, the twist
Movie-star paper dolls
Distinctive toys and games that are no longer made
The early days of TV: "Howdy-Doody," "Mouseketeers"
Premiums given away by the cereal companies
The cardboard box panels that offered them
Unusual cigarette lighters

We had better stop here, or the rest of this book will never be written. Keep thinking; you'll come up with dozens more. There will always be more. Interesting, quaint second-hand items, to buy, sell, and collect.

Direct Sources

The most important single thing you can do to find direct sources is to buy all your local newspapers, daily or weekly, as often as they are available and covering as wide an area as you can get to easily. If you live in a large city, it might be two or three dailies and a weekly neighborhood paper. Don't forget the heavy Sunday papers, sometimes the best information source of all. In a small town, it might be just a county weekly paper and a daily from the nearest city. Buy them all and read the ads—all of them. Read the notices for "Community Affairs." Go through those papers carefully. They will tell you about prime sources.

RUMMAGE AND BAZAAR SALES

These are our favorites, and they might become yours too. The unexpected often turns up. And that's what you're looking for—the things few people will look for there, because they are not expected to be there. Among the many finds we've made are:

> An old silver candlestick hiding under tarnish
> An expensive lucite handbag on a table covered with imitation leather bags (each with a broken handle
> Many pure silk scarves
> Some old magazines with signed illustrations
> An antique wedding dress

Get there early. A line usually forms an hour or so before the opening. And don't be discouraged if each sale is not a gold mine. There will be enough that are.

THRIFT SHOPS

Everybody has his own steady sources under this heading: the Salvation Army, Goodwill, Planned Parenthood, etc. You'll find many listed in the Yellow Pages. But, please, be careful. Everything there will have been priced by an amateur, a permanent volunteer. Some things will be very much overpriced; others will be real bargains. It all depends on the taste of the volunteer. Don't get carried away.

HOUSE SALES

Professionally run tag sales are usually advertised in local papers. But for sales run by the householders themselves you will have to keep an eye out for signs posted on trees and lampposts. Ask your friends and family to tell you of any they hear of. Again, get there early, at least half an hour before official opening time. The early bird catches the great buys, and that's exactly what you want. The good Lord alone knows what has been resting in any basement for a long while. It's your job to find out. And bring your own wrappings, bags, and boxes. You'll seldom find any at the sale.

OTHER FLEAS

Block parties, street fairs, whatever: They are all flea markets. And all good sources.

Dom enjoys dealing in bronze medals; the more unusual the subject of the medal, the better he likes it. All our local dealers save whatever medals they find for Dom.

"Look at this, Dom." Harry was all smiles. "Read the inscription on this medal. It commemorates the Austrian army's Turkish campaign in World War I. How far out can you get? I bet you've never seen another one like it."

"Never seen anything like it?" Dom replied. "I've seen it and sold it, two years ago. Where did you find it?"

"At a block party, just yesterday. Well, I guess you aren't interested in buying."

"Who says I'm not interested? How much are you asking for it?"

"Take it for $8. I paid $6, but I thought it would be new to you."

"Here's your $8. I sold it once, I can sell it again. Round and round it goes."

RUNNERS

Like a few other dealers, Harry sometimes acts as a runner for his dealer friends. A runner is someone who buys with a specific dealer in mind. A full-time runner has no shop and doesn't rent space anywhere, anytime. He operates out of his back pocket. He is constantly on the move, from market to market, from shop to shop. buying only what he knows he can sell to a dealer who specializes in that particular item. Runners are a very good source of supply. When a runner approaches you for the first time, buy what he offers, even if it's not the bargain of the year. Tell him exactly what you do want and what you want to pay for it. He's bound to turn up something. And he comes to you. It's a great time-saver.

Antique Shops

Yes, you can buy and buy well in many antique shops. The shop owner often has items that don't fit in with his stock or his decor or won't appeal to his customers. Why did he buy them in the first place? They may have been part of a package deal. His whole shop is devoted to Victorian fashions. Very posh. The collection he bought last week came in two trunks—one large for dresses, and one full of small compartments for accessories. He can't use the trunks, but you can. He gets rid of them; you get a bargain. Everyone is happy. Maybe one of those trunks has a stack of old fashion magazines lying at the bottom. Again, you've made a good find. Keep going back. Perhaps he'll remember to call you when more of the same turns up.

Mail Order

Do you enjoy spending a quiet evening at home? Put your feet up on a hassock, relax, reach for a recent copy of an antique trade paper, and dive into those classified ads. They go on and on, page after page. Be persistent. Look for what you know you can sell in your locality that's being offered at a wholesale price. The ads originate in every state, including Alaska. And what's a drag there may be a hot number where you are. You can trust most of the dealers who advertise in these papers. They are interested in repeat customers. And you have the protection of being able to return, for a full refund, whatever might turn out to be not as it was advertised. Here are some wholesale lots we recently read about:

100 pieces of railroad paper items	$ 4.00
10 old Betty Boop charms	15.00
35 old pictorial cigar bands	2.00
567 old glass marbles	19.00
14 advertising bottle openers	28.00

Where can you find these trade papers? Just drop them a note, tell them you're a dealer, and ask for a free sample copy. We're sure you will want to subscribe after your first reading.

American Collector
Box A
Reno, Nevada, 98506

The Antique Trader
Box 1050
Dubuque, Iowa 52001

Collectors News
606 8th St.
Grundy Center, Iowa 50638

JUST PLAIN PEOPLE

Many people who want to sell their own things don't want to bother holding a public sale. How do you reach them? Advertise! The cheapest method of advertising is to put a large sign on your table. Use a thick Magic Marker and make the letters large. Here are some effective table signs we've seen and used:

WE BUY ANYTHING OLD.
ARE YOU SELLING? WE ARE BUYING!
WE HAVE THE CASH, WHAT ARE YOU SELLING?

You will want to put an ad in your local paper, in the

classified section under "Wanted to Buy." Make your ad short and sweet:

WANTED. *We pay cash for anything old.*
Call *** **** *now.*

Even if the responses are few in number, you can make those few result in terrific buys.

Keep working at all these sources and you will never have to worry about finding enough merchandise to sell.

7

What Can You Sell?

What can you sell? It's easy enough to answer, "Almost anything, as long as it's old and interesting." But what exactly? Here's a list of things that have worked for us.

Pots and pans: The older and more seasoned they are, the better the taste of the food.

Alligator and snakeskin handbags: Very much the fashion and no guilt feelings about slaughtering endangered species. (The same is true of old fur, a good buy if well cared for and in good shape.)

Lamps and mirrors: Two of the most salable items you'll ever carry.

Old games and toys: There seems to be a natural curiosity about what other generations had fun with.

Vintage clothing: The quality of the cloth, the basic construction, the care with which the details were handled make it obvious why these are so popular.

Old furniture: For the same reasons as old clothes: quality materials and craftsmanship.

Old books: Be careful. Some subjects are a lot more salable than others. Stick to cookbooks, humor, catalogues, craft books, and those illustrated by famous artists.

Used records: Anything "popular" that the buyer can't find new in a record shop. Stay away from the classics.

Baskets: The most beautiful way to store and display almost anything that doesn't need to be covered.

Scrapbooks and diaries: Desirable as social history and sometimes as just fun reading and browsing.

Clocks and watches: Be sure they work. The cost of repairs can be more than their value.

Old frames: To match the style of whatever is going inside them.

Large pottery planters: Popular at the turn of the century and now when houseplants are in.

Vintage trunks and suitcases: There is always a crying need for large storage units in modern homes and apartments.

Old food and tobacco tins: Large and small, they are great as kitchen canisters. You can't find more colorful storage boxes than these.

You'll constantly run across new items. Don't hesitate; gather them up. As our fellow dealer, Dom, says: "Somebody loved it once, somebody else can love it again . . . and again." With this attitude, you'll never run out of merchandise or have to ask that nightmare question: "What else is there left to sell?"

Below we've listed 288 different items we found in flea markets we've visited and worked at. Remember, the greater the variety, the more interested your customer will be. Just try to get it all as old as it can possibly be.

Books

Children's
Art
Travelogues
Western history
Big Little Books
Cookery

Boy Scouts
Aviation
Ocean liners
Racing
Gambling
Astrology

Those illustrated by famous artists:

Christy
Gibson
Parrish
Fisher
Rockwell

Greenaway
Rackham
Wyeth
O'Neill
Leyendecker

China

Salts and peppers
Roseville pottery
Fiestaware
Limoges
Pickard
Rookwood pottery
Tiles
Teapots
Toby jugs
Tobacco jars
Hummels
Beer steins
"Old Sleepy Eye"
Tea sets
Buffalo pottery
Kewpie china

Mustache mugs
Cups and saucers
Figural cookie jars
"Occupied Japan"
Shawnee pottery
Baby-feeding bowls
Cloisonné
Flow blue pottery
Ironstone
Lamps
Nippon
Royal Doulton
R. S. Prussia
Railroad china
"Sunbonnet Babies"
    china

Fashions

Dolls' clothes
Hatpins
Quilts
Fancy buttons
Powder compacts
Fancy pocket mirrors
Pincushions
Watch fobs
Crocheted doilies
Tablecloths
Bedspreads
Dresses
Skirts
Store manikins
Hats
Lace collars and cuffs
Military uniforms
Costume jewelry
Costumes
Cowboy shirts

Ski sweaters
Embroideries
Kimonos
Smoking jackets
Belt buckles
Shoe buckles
Fancy umbrella handles
Fans
Tops
Silk scarves
Shawls
Handkerchiefs
Beaded bags
Alligator bags
High-button shoes
Children's clothes
Canes
Fine jewelry in gold,
   silver, ivory

Furnishings

Wicker accessories
Radios
Picture frames
Sewing baskets
Oak chairs
Ice-cream-parlor chairs
Music boxes
Oak sewing machine
   tables
Trunks
Bookends

Small rugs
Clocks
Wooden boxes
Pipe racks
Minicabinets
Printers' trays
Small end tables
Dolls' furniture
Children's furniture
Doorstops
Small bath fixtures

Glass

Depression
Carnival
Cambridge
Akro agate
Milk glass
Children's toy dishes
Heisey
Fostoria
Cut glass
Pattern
Victorian colored
Fruit jars
Avon containers
Lamps
Whiskey bottles
Perfume bottles
Greentown
Medicine bottles
Salt dips
Lemonade sets
Brides' baskets
Condiment sets

Mustard jars
Candlesticks
Ink bottles
Goblets
Fancy pickle jars
Animals
Orange and lemon
  juicers
Marbles
Beads
Christmas ornaments
Barbers' bottles
Paperweights
Inkwells
Stained-glass windows
Candy containers
Toothpick holders
Spoon holders
Stretch
Cranberry
Soda bottles

Hardware

Small bronze statues
Telephones
Small business machines
Tape measures
Advertising rulers
Cigar cutters
Fountain pens
Keys
Locks
Scales

Medallions
Medals
Coffee mills
Metal lamps
Silver frames
Tea sets
Candlesticks
Thimbles
Scissors
Spoons

Hardware (cont.)

Lunch boxes
Dinner pails
Microscopes
Bits and spurs
Ice cream molds
Tools
Knobs
Tobacco tins
Food tins

Handles
Kitchen utensils
Auto accessories
Insulators
Razors
Pocketknives
Railroad artifacts
Cameras
Bricks

Magazines

Pulps
Gardening
Women's
Camera Work
Playboy
Radio
National Geographic

Fashion
Food
Comics
Life
Movie
Saturday Evening Post
Harper's Monthly

Miscellaneous Collectibles

World's Fair souvenirs
Shirley Temple
    memorabilia
Dolls
Banks
Toys
Miniatures
Coins
Indian relics
Records
Guns
Beer cans
Soda cans
Souvenir spoons

Soda fountain dispensers
Shoehorns
Bottle openers
Fancy corkscrews
Campaign ribbons
Political premiums
Cracker-Jack prizes
Games
Advertising pocket
    mirrors
Beer scrapers
Change trays
Disneyana
Police badges

Miscellaneous Collectibles (cont.)

Lionel trains
Stamps
Salesmen's samples
Elk's souvenirs
Masonic souvenirs
Talcum powder shakers
Figural napkin rings
Seashells
Cartoon characters

Snuffboxes
Flags
Bookmarks
Silk woven pictures
Punchboards
Sports stars
Movie stars
Buttons
Political buttons

Paper

Dixie Cup lids
Paper dolls
Diaries
Catalogues
Postcards
Valentines
Playing cards
Premium cards
Trade cards
Menus
Theatrical programs
Railroad timetables
Ships' passenger lists
Maps
Brochures
Advertising labels
Die cuts
Tobacco tags

Photographs
Stock certificates
Photograph albums
Stereo viewcards
Calendars
Blotters
Advertising counter
   signs
Matchbook covers
Cigar labels
Cigar bands
Billheads
Repair manuals
Songsheets
Posters
Prints
Scrapbooks

Records (out of print)

Jazz
Famous popular
   performers
Popular songs

Original cast albums of
   Broadway and Holly-
   wood musicals

8

Everything Has a Price

The Great Unknown

We've all had advice on how to price our merchandise. *Either:* "Buy one of the famous price guides. Everything is listed alphabetically. Just look up your item and you know the price to charge." *Or:* "Before you begin selling, visit the flea markets and see what prices the dealers are charging and then you will also know how much to charge."

But the only truly workable answer we know is the one Harry gave to a woman who walked up to him one Sunday. She waited for a spare moment between customers.

"Maybe you can help me," she said. "I have a lot of things, maybe twenty cartons, old dishes and such that my aunt left me. I'd like to sell them."

"Sure," Harry replied. "Tell me where you live and I'll come down, look them over and make you an offer."

"Oh no, I didn't mean that I want you to buy them. I just thought you could tell me how much to price them. After all, I don't want to give them away. I'd rather bring them all to a flea market and sell them myself."

Harry smiled. "I'm sorry, dear, but it cost me a lot of time and money to learn what I know, and I'm not about to give it away. I guess you'll have to do it the hard way just like the rest of us poor mortals. Since you haven't paid any money for what's in the cartons, you can't lose. Just price each item at how much you would pay for it if you were buying."

"But I don't know what it's worth," she insisted. And shaking her head, she wandered away.

Harry knew she would never turn up at a flea market as a dealer. Making money has nothing to do with worrying about worth. The ultimate worth of any secondhand object is the amount of money anyone is willing to *pay you* for it. This is *not* what the price tag would read on the item in a beautiful antique shop and not the price the same object brought at a famous auction house. It's the price your customer is willing actually to hand you.

Never pay attention to what other dealers are charging for their stock. As Dom says, shaking his head sagely: "Paper takes ink, and they can tag whatever price they please, but that doesn't mean anyone is paying that number."

Then how do you price your goods? Read on.

One, Two, Three

You should be using a three-times markup on items that cost you less than $5. Use a two-times markup on items that cost over $5.

Item	Price You Paid	Price You Tag	Your Bottom Line
1930s pure silk scarf, geometric design	$ 2.00	$ 6.00	$ 5.00
Old pocket knife, cover has ad for cigars	1.00	3.00	2.50
Old children's book with good illustrations	4.00	12.00	10.00
Matchholder, heavy silver shaped like a high-button shoe	6.00	12.00	10.00
Primitive wooden coffee mill	15.00	30.00	25.00
Stretch glass bowl	10.00	20.00	18.00

This method of pricing will cover all your expenses and still leave you a good profit. You see how important it is to buy for the right price. Go back and reread Chapter 5, How to Buy. Buying and pricing go hand in hand.

How Much Would You Pay?

There are times when the above pattern of pricing won't apply:

1. When you are selling your freebies. It's yours or it's been given to you.
2. When you buy a large number of items for one lump sum.
3. When, oh lucky day, you find a fantastic bargain. A two- or three-time markup would be silly.

Nothing about the flea market business is automatic. Be flexible about your pricing and everything else. Here are some bargains we were lucky to find. And believe us, it doesn't happen too often.

Item	Price Paid	Price Tagged	Our Bottom Line
Black Kewpie doll with original label	$ 5.00	$65.00	$55.00
Celluloid bank, elephant-shaped	1.00	20.00	18.00
Hopalong Cassidy roller skates, 1950s, original box	12.00	75.00	65.00

In pricing the above we used Harry's method. We held each item in our hands, looked at it hard, and said: "If we were customers and wanted this to add to our collections, how much would we be willing to pay for it?" And we came up with the above prices. All three items sold in a reasonable length of time at our bottom-line prices.

As you work more flea markets you will be learning about new-to-you merchandise items and about what your customers will pay for them. That knowledge is your stock-in-trade. It takes time and money to learn it, but once you have it you will never lose it.

Never Worry About Worth

Susan was really upset. Alex tried to comfort her.

"You should be smiling, not crying."

"How can you say that? Look at all the money we lost."

"But we didn't lose anything. How much did you pay for that tiny cloisonné box?"

"$1.50."

"And how much did you get for it?"

"$22.00."

"Then how can you say we lost? I'd say you made $20.50 cash money."

"But the dealer who paid me $22 for it sold it for $118

today, right here at this market. I didn't know it was worth that much."

"What does it matter? You made money, and the dealer who bought it from you made money. That's all that matters. That's what makes the flea market. As long as we make a good profit, we're on the right road."

9

Make Me an Offer

The Give and Take of Bargaining

Bargaining is fun. Customer to dealer, dealer to customer. You find yourself playing a game of verbal tennis. Many people shop at flea markets just because they love to bargain. Where else could they find dealers so flexible with prices?

There are dealers who are superstars at the game. They take it seriously. But money is fun. We have fun talking about it and handling it. It's a feeling we have in common with you, and that you share with your customers.

A pleasant middle-aged woman stood facing us across our table. She was holding two pieces of very old sheet music. They both had beautifully designed covers, clowns and other circus motifs.

One was priced at $3 and the other at $4. "I can't believe it," the woman said. "Just a few years ago, I was buying any piece of sheet music for 50¢ apiece, 'take your pick.'"

"We know just how you feel," we sympathized. "We are great coffee drinkers, and for the longest time, we paid a dollar a pound. Now every time we market, it's $3 or $4 a pound."

"Oh, you're right," our customer sighed, "everything costs more."

"Look," we said, "both pieces add up to $7. Take them for $6. Maybe that will help."

"Yes," she agreed, "that sounds good. I'll take them for $6. And thank you."

You'll find that most of the give and take is pleasant. But sometimes a dealer works too hard at bargaining and meets his match.

"That's a nice pair of binoculars," one customer remarked, as he casually laid them down in their handmade walnut box.

"The best, made for the Kaiser's army. The finest pair I've seen in forty years of flea markets." Dom never passes up a chance to throw a sales pitch.

"Well, $90 is just too much for them."

"So, I'm here. Talk to me and I'll listen."

"They're worth $60 to me. That's my final offer."

"You must be joking. Everyone knows $140 would be a fair price. So I've already come down $50. What more could you ask?"

"Listen, I've got $65 in my pocket. Cash money. Take it or leave it."

"Of course, cash money. What else? Coin, maybe? Look, I like you. You have good taste. It takes someone like you to appreciate this fine pair. Take them for $75. I'll even throw in the box."

"Throw it in? The box belongs with the binoculars. It was made for them. I still stand by my $65 offer. What do you say?"

"I'll take it," Dom decided quickly. He began packing them carefully. "You sure got a good buy."

"It's a great buy. They really caught my eye. If you had

kept to your original $90 price, I would have ended up paying it. I wanted these binoculars. And you're right, they are the finest I've seen."

When should you be flexible? And when should you stand firm? There is no simple answer. Each situation calls for a different solution. Ask yourself these questions:

1. Just how anxious am I to sell that piece?
2. Have I had it a long time?
3. Do most customers just ignore it?
4. Is it getting handled too much and beginning to look shabby?
5. Do I need cash for that great buy that might turn up next week?

Think it over. Maybe Dom did the wise thing. Perhaps the customer was boasting. Remember, $65 in your pocket is worth more than $90 in the bush.

Be on Your Guard

Janet prefers to buy in quantity whenever possible, but so do her customers. And what they love to buy are the art deco pieces she tries very hard to find for them.

A young antique dealer was surprised to find she had three vintage pieces which she was displaying at his neighborhood block party.

1. Small dressing table, completely covered with mirrors	$65.00
2. Crystal perfume bottle, shaped like a triangle	12.00
3. Heavy glass ashtray, royal blue color	8.00
	$85.00

After looking at all three items very carefully, he called Janet over to the dressing table.

"This is a lovely little table," he said. "I can offer you $55 for it. The perfume bottle looks perfect sitting on one corner of it, and that adds $10, for a $63 total. I'll also take the ashtray—the color adds pizzazz, don't you think? So $6 more comes to $68 altogether." Taking out his checkbook, the young dealer began filling in the date on the top check.

Janet mentally added and subtracted, very fast. And decided to have some fun. As she subtracted items, she added dollars.

"Well, suppose we leave out the ashtray. That would bring the total to $76," said Janet as she put it back in its original place. "And let's not complicate matters with the perfume bottle. I don't think it looks good right there anyway. That leaves us with an even $88 for the dressing table."

The customer laughed. "OK, OK, you win, but I do want the dressing table. How much do I make the check out for?"

"For $60.00," replied Janet. "That's my bottom line." And there the sale ended.

Janet is very quick, but Harry isn't. He thinks hard and slow. He pauses before answering any question about price. Harry's response to the tricky young dealer would have been a different one, but an honest one.

"Now look here, young man, you're just too fast for me. Do you see the tag on each piece? Well, you tell me what it is you are interested in and I'll tell you my best price for it, and you can say yes or no, and if it's yes, we have a deal."

"OK," the young man might say, "I'm sorry. Let's begin again. I would like the dressing table. Can you take $60 for it?"

"I sure can," said Harry. "Sold for $60.00." Harry likes to keep things simple.

Your Bottom Line

Do you know what it is on every piece in your stock? Your very bottom line, the lowest price you'll take for any of it, no matter what the circumstances.

If your answer is no, you had better go over your merchandise and decide what exactly is your bottom line. Go back to Chapter 8, Everything Has a Price, and you will see on the charts how we calculate our bottom line. Try it on your stock. You need to be able to think fast enough to be in step with all your customers. About half of them will pay the price tagged. They don't enjoy bargaining; they aren't interested in give and take. But you have to be ready for the other half, the game players.

And you will enjoy it. If you didn't love dealing with people, you wouldn't be in the flea market in the first place.

You *deal in* merchandise, your stock. But you also *deal with* people: browsers and buyers. Be ready for almost anything and enjoy the unexpected—it never bores.

Yes, You Can Say No

You can, we know you can, if you're confident. And after reading this book, that's exactly what you will be. The merchandise is yours. You can choose to accept an offer or refuse to discuss it at all.

If you refuse an offer, you should have a good reason:

1. It's the first time you've put that item on display. Give it a chance.
2. You know your tagged price is low. Why should you go lower?
3. You don't like dealing with this particular customer and want him to just go away.
4. A steady, generous customer has asked you to buy any of such an item you can find for him.

We've learned to be firm, and so will you. Your customers will trust and admire you all the more for it. Being firm will make your bargaining experiences a lot more fun for you.

10

What's in a Name?

A Flea by Any Other Name . . .

There would seem to be no limit to the imagination of flea market operators. They want their markets to have distinctive names that will stay with you.

Here are some of the names we've seen on our travels, visiting flea markets:

Antique Extravaganza	Collector's Market
Bazaar	Antique Mini-Mart
Antique Fair and Flea Market	Thieves Market
County Fair	Open Market
Antique Market	Antiques Exposition
Swap Meet	Americana
	Super-Flea

There are thousands of markets all over the country. Whether they are large or small, their owners try hard to rent space to as many dealers as they have room for. Before

Gate   *Food*

Covered Shed

The mammoth market with its acres of parked cars and dealers' tables

The neighborhood market, weekdays a parking lot

you take the plunge, visit as many as you can—the one that's around the corner, down the block, the other side of town, or at your county fairgrounds.

Promoters are always busy. They put on shows in many towns and cities, every week or two, covering as large an area as possible. Some carry on business statewide, and a few work an entire section of the country—all of New England, for example. Each has his own distinctive style. If you find a promoter you like and whose style appeals to you, stay with him. He's a real find. And as a steady renter, you'll get better treatment, such as a choice spot at all his shows.

Where to Sell What

The public comes to a flea market to find a large selection of whatever it wants to buy. So be smart and choose a market where the dealers are selling your type of merchandise. If you visit a medium-sized flea market (under fifty tables) where most of the dealers are selling antique jewelry and Victorian clothing, it's not for you if your merchandise dates from the 1930s and 1940s. Keep looking until you find a market where a large amount of your type of merchandise is displayed.

When you rent space in one of the really large annual markets, say 300 to 500 dealers, ask the promoter to place you with other dealers whose stock relates to yours. Interested customers will find their way to your table if a group of dealers pulls together.

Are you dealing in advertising material? Or in any of the items listed under Miscellaneous Collectibles in Chapter 7, What Can You Sell? Then you should certainly show up at the many "collectibles shows." They may be held in sports arenas, convention centers, or the ballrooms of large hotels. But, one and all, they are still flea markets.

When you visit any market, go in the middle of the afternoon and look at the crowds. If there are no crowds, don't waste time even looking. Do those crowds look like the kinds of people you want to deal with, the sort who would be interested in what you're selling? If the answer is yes, don't hesitate. Rent a booth and open your business.

The Best One for Now

If your business is new, treat it like a newborn baby, gently and carefully. Be patient. It takes a long time for a baby to stop crawling and start walking. But then, before you know it, he's running and jumping.

Start small, at a small, successful market where the rent is low. Learn what you can. Sell what you can. And keep improving your stock. Small markets are more flexible; they're easier for a beginner to settle into and gradually build up a personal following of customers.

Keep as close to home as possible, and be good to yourself. The less *extra* work you do, the better those profit dollars will look.

How to Move Up

It's time to move up when you've outgrown that first market. And you've outgrown it when:

1. You find you are doing more business each Sunday than any other dealer there
2. Your customers ask why they didn't see you at the most recent large antique show held in your town or city
3. Your stock looks better and better to you, while every other dealer's stock remains the same

Be ready for the big time. Now that you know your way around a flea market, it's much easier to move. But before you do move, make sure your favorite customers know where you're going. Write it out for them: name, address, and hours. Those customers are important. Wherever you go to sell, bring them along. You want to add to your list of customers, not just trade in one group for another.

See that your merchandise includes a few show stoppers—the beautiful, unusual, or rare items no one can resist looking at. They may cost more than you usually pay for stock, but in this case, they are not merely stock. They are attention grabbers that say "STOP" to the crowds right there in front of your table. Once the browsers do stop and you have their attention, the rest is up to you. Put a high, but intelligent, price on your stop signs. You want to keep them as long as you can, but you don't want to scare anyone away with outrageous prices on anything you are displaying.

Check your supplies. Are they too shabby for the better market? Do you need a new table cover or even a new table? It's no trouble to brighten things. Keep on moving up. Never let your stock get stale. The more your business grows, the higher your profits go.

What the Market Provides

You pay rent for each day you are selling in any flea market. What exactly are you paying for? It can differ widely from market to market. Some promoters have printed contracts; you sign and he signs. Make sure you have a copy with his signature on it to keep for your records. Before you sign any contract, read it carefully. Put on your glasses and read all the fine print. If there is no printed contract, you'll have to ask the market owner specific questions. Be sure you get straight answers to each of the following:

INDOOR SHOWS

1. Exactly what size is your space? How many feet and inches? (Who knows? You might have room for an extra small table.)
2. Where will your booth be? (Don't let him place you under a balcony, behind a column, or in any hidden spot. You want the center of action, not the backwater.)
3. Are there any electrical outlets in your space? (You

know the lighting will be terrible. Bring your own adjustable table lights and extension cords.)

4. Will he provide you with tables and chairs? If so, how many? (Bring a chair for every helper you have along, or you'll find yourself standing all day.)

5. Can you bring your own table covers? (His will be an awful shade of mustard or khaki; yours is lovely, fresh, and clean, possibly a printed bed sheet.)

6. Will he provide any security? And what exactly does he call security? (If the show lasts longer than one day and you have anything really valuable at your booth, take it home with you each night. Better tired than sorry.)

7. How much advertising and promotion does he promise? (Make sure you check these promises. If they turn out to be fantasies, you'll know for next time.)

OUTDOOR SHOWS

Questions 1, 2, and 7 are the same for outdoor shows. Tables and chairs are rarely provided outdoors, but rents are usually cheaper. Be sure to ask the next question:

8. Is there a rain date? (If there isn't and it does rain, you might lose your rent money, if paid in advance.)

What your rent really covers, besides the practical items we've listed above, is the people who walk through the gate. How many? What kind? Will they keep coming? If the answers to these questions are the ones you want to hear, then your rent money is well spent.

11

Props

Bring a Friend

The most important prop you will ever have in the flea market is a friend. He or she can be literally your best friend or a member of your family. You can begin your business with a partner, with each of you bringing his own merchandise, selling it at the same table, and sharing rent and traveling expenses. In a pinch you can hire a teenager, someone you know well, to come and help you for a day.

You need that friend to pitch in with the physical work—unloading, unpacking, and arranging your stock. Someone to help with selling when the market gets busy. Someone who will take turns going for coffee, eating lunch, using the restrooms. Everyone needs moral support on a busy day of dealing with crowds of people. It's a good idea for you to have a friend to lean on.

Harry doesn't have a "friend." He has many friends, sometimes as many as four or five men, elderly retirees like himself. They sit together behind his tables and reminisce about the "old neighborhood." We sometimes eavesdrop and wonder where that neighborhood actually was. In New York, Chicago, perhaps some European city? Harry's friends cover for him. Their presence allows him to wander around the market when things are slow, to share stories and gossip with other dealers. They watch his stock, sell when necessary, and pack up at the end of the day, say good-bye to Harry and each other, and wander off, each to his own home.

Save Your Paper Bags

It's important to save paper bags and to be as economical as you can with your props. And by props we mean anything you bring and use that isn't for sale. It's not a part of your stock; it's a prop that helps to sell that stock. The less money you spend on these things, the more you will have available to invest in merchandise.

1. *Paper bags:* Save all you can get your hands on regardless of size. Don't worry about them being used; they'll match the flea market style.
2. *Shopping bags:* Gather up a good supply, paper or plastic, through your own purchases and those of generous friends.
3. *Shallow display cases:* If you are selling anything small and valuable, particularly jewelry, these are a necessity. Made of glass and aluminum, they come with lock and key and are easily portable. You can lay them down right on top of your table. Everything is visible, but out of reach. They cost anywhere from $20 to $40 each, and are advertised in the trade papers listed in Chapter 6, Where Does It All Come From?
4. *Tables:* The best flea market tables are made of lightweight aluminum. Six feet long by three feet wide, they fold up to bridge table size (three feet square). Avoid

the heavy metal folding tables; it takes two people to lift them. The aluminum table sells for $35 to $45, and you can get one at any department store. That's also the place to pick up an inexpensive bridge table if you don't already have an old one at home. Try the secondhand shops for good buys in portable tables and folding chairs. New, such chairs are very inexpensive in late summer when discount stores like to clear out their stock of beach chairs. Make sure the chairs are comfortable and cool.

5. *Table covers:* Whether your tables are new or secondhand, you'll need attractive covers for them. Make sure those covers are long enough to reach the floor. That way your cartons, bags, and so on will be hidden from view and not distract from the stock on your table. Think in those terms when you choose a cover. Avoid wild, garish patterns. Remember, the cover is only a background. Avoid white or very pale colors that will soon look grubby. The new printed bed sheets in the double-bed size are perfect. Indian bedspreads have the added advantages of being inexpensive and very sturdy. If you can possibly use anything you have at home, do so by all means. The less spent, the better.

6. *Display racks:* If you are selling old things, make sure your display pieces date from around the same period. Wooden cheese boxes, old cigar boxes, old portable magazine stands and music stands are a few of the things we've seen used by dealers. Any time you come upon an old store going out of business, check to see if they are selling or discarding their old wire racks. These weigh nothing and can hold a lot of small paper goods or dozens of scarves. Just be careful that your racks or boxes enhance the merchandise you are selling. Don't let them detract from or cover up too much of your stock.

7. *Hardware, paper, and other necessities:* (See checklist page 69).

Displaying Your Stock

The first thing to decide is how you are going to set up your tables. Here are diagrams of two different styles. You can choose to follow either or to create your own. You can vary your setup from week to week until you find the one most suited to your business.

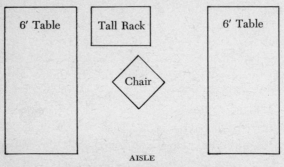

DIAGRAM A has the advantage of having all of your stock open to viewing and handling. It's ideal if you concentrate on a low-cost, high-volume business.

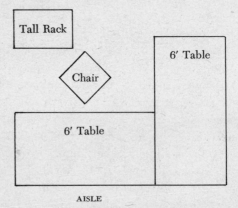

DIAGRAM B allows you to be flexible. Items that should be handled go across the front table right on the aisle and on the front half of your second table. The stock on the back half of that table and your rack are visible, but can't be touched unless you decide to hand them to your customer.

In general, it's wise to put small items up front on your tables, large items toward the back. If you have postcards or any other stock that requires a lot of viewing time from the customer, cluster them off to the side. You don't want that customer blocking the view of crowds walking down the

Every square inch matters. Get as much mileage as possible from your tabletop display:

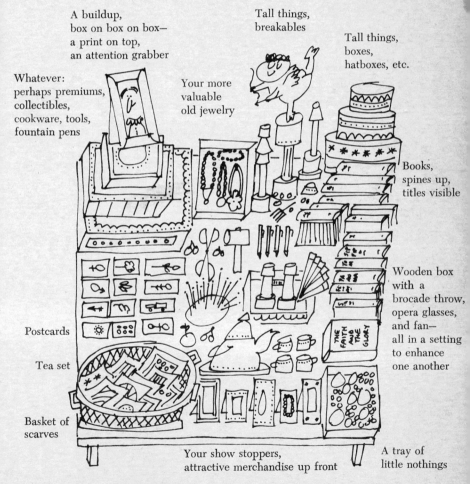

A buildup,
box on box on box—
a print on top,
an attention grabber

Tall things,
breakables

Tall things,
boxes,
hatboxes, etc.

Whatever:
perhaps premiums,
collectibles,
cookware, tools,
fountain pens

Your more
valuable
old jewelry

Books,
spines up,
titles visible

Wooden box
with a
brocade throw,
opera glasses,
and fan—
all in a setting
to enhance
one another

Postcards

Tea set

Basket of
scarves

Your show stoppers,
attractive merchandise up front

A tray of
little nothings

Your little nothings, which will be somethings for the customer, should be to the sides. They could be game tokens, old dress patterns, pins, scarves, labels.

Something tall—
a ladder
(each rung can
display wares),
a rack,
even a tall stool

If there's a lot to look at, it's worth the browser's time. You sell, of course; but let the merchandise sell too.

aisle. And remember to put those show stoppers where they will do you the most good. Stand in the aisle and look head-on at your booth. The spot your eye hits first is the place for them.

Try not to be too neat in your arrangement of stock. People love to dig in, fish around, and come up with a prize. Make it easy for them. Make it fun. They'll show their appreciation by buying even more.

Your Cash Register

It's right there. On you. Keep your money in your skirt or trouser pockets. Using a cashbox or a handbag is too dangerous. If you can put it down, someone else can pick it up. Try to buy clothing with lots of deep pockets. You can keep large bills in shirt pockets, fives and singles in pants and skirts. Leaving one pocket free for change. And bring lots of change. If you've priced everything in multiples of 25¢, quarters are the only coins you'll have to worry about. Get a $10 roll of them at the bank. You'll also need at least $30 in singles, ten $5 bills, and a few tens. Of course, the first customer of the day may hand you a $100 bill for a $5 purchase, but it's not very likely. And you can always ask him to pick out more items, and then you'll have enough change for him.

Flea Market Checklist

Use it every time you work a flea market. Once you are stationed at your booth, you can't run out and get what you need. This checklist will make sure you have it all.

1. Change (coins and bills)
2. Tables
3. Chairs
4. Table covers
5. Racks
6. Display boxes
7. Shopping bags
8. Paper bags
9. Newspaper for wrapping
10. Small notebook
11. Pens and pencils
12. Masking tape
13. Scotch tape
14. Tacks
15. Tarpaulins in case of rain
16. White cardboards for signs
17. Wide felt-tipped pen for signs
18. Receipt book
19. Scissors
20. Razor blades
21. Tape measure
22. Price tags
23. Penknife
24. Light screwdriver
25. Hammer
26. Pliers

And last, but not least, lunch—enough food and drink for you and everyone you bring with you. Although plenty of food is for sale at almost any flea market, brown-bagging it can mean lower operating expenses for the day. And you want to take home as many profit dollars as you possibly can.

12

How to Sell

The Easy Part

It is easy. As simple as talking. And that's all it is—talking
—about the things you like. The stock you're selling must hold
some meaning for you or you wouldn't have bought it for
resale in the first place. Of course, the profit motive comes
first. "If you can make money on it, buy it." But you do re-
spond to what it is you are selling. And your customer also
responds—that is what you both have in common. He'll stop,
pick it up, ask the price, talk about it. And when you answer,
you will be selling. Make it a pleasant experience for both
of you.

Dealers say it's the crowds, the customers that make flea
markets interesting, each one looking for things he can't buy
anywhere else, looking for a bargain, a good buy.

Customers feel it's the dealers that make the flea market,

each with his or her own taste, choice of stock, manner of talking.

Susan and Alex like to soft sell. The customer has to almost beg to buy. Susan *loves* everything she owns and can't bear to part with any of it. Alex must persuade her while the customer waits, hoping Alex succeeds so that he can buy the dolls' china tea set for his wife. She collects them and it's hard to find one in mint condition, original box and all. Is it a game among the three of them? Is the tea set all the more valuable for having to be begged for? Is Susan serious? Then why do she and Alex work in the flea market at all? No one knows. But it's interesting to watch them. Most important of all, Susan and Alex make money. Each Sunday, spring, summer and fall, they gross $300 to $400, half of it net profit.

Every successful dealer has his own style. It's something that develops on its own. It can't be manufactured. As you begin to talk and sell, watch the customer. Be guided by his or her reaction. Before long, you too will have developed a certain style. It won't be Susan's or Harry's. It will be yours.

Keep Adding On

How many times can you turn a single purchase into a multiple one? The next time a customer chooses one item and says, "I'll take it, wrap it up," take it out of his hand and put it down behind the table. Keep talking about his choice, how clever he is to collect something so interesting. What good taste she has to choose the loveliest one of its kind on your table. While you're talking pick up a variation on the same type of merchandise. Point out its great qualities, how much it complements the one already chosen, how well they go together. Offer to give him a good buy if he takes them both. Choose your own way to do it, but keep adding on. You can only handle X number of sales per day. Try for $X \times 2$, or 3, or even 4. It's a fun game and a profitable one.

Dealing with Dealers

You don't have to think about "add ons" when dealing with other dealers. They almost always buy in volume, which is why we all like to sell to one another. It's well worth the discount you give them. How much of a discount is up to you, not them. It's your choice. Try to have an obvious price tag on each item, the best indication a dealer has that he is indeed getting a discount. It also inspires trust in the heart of the retail customer. He or she knows the original quoted price is the same regardless of who is asking.

Think twice when you are selling to a dealer who is displaying his goods at the same place you are. If he walks over to your table before the market opens to the public and picks out all your show stoppers, the best you have, think before you sell. His stock will look much better, but yours will suddenly look less so. What can you say? Tell him to come back at the end of the day, and if you still have them, you'll be happy to sell. Be pleasant, but firm, and you can't lose.

See Us Next Week

Once you're established, you'll remember to finish each sale by saying, "See us next week." And you'll make sure to tell each new customer:

"We always have fresh, new stock."
"We might have more of what you like at home."
"Now that we know what you collect, we'll make an effort to get more."

Steady customers will see you next week, week after week. As those steady customers grow in number, your gross sales will also grow, week after week.

13

How Much Money?

Are You Making Any?

Only your notebooks will tell you if you're making money.
Here's a simple, quick way to find out:

1. Buy three small spiral pads.
2. Label the first "outgo." That's what it is, a record of all
   your money that "goes out," that you spend. Divide
   each page into five columns, label them, and fill in the
   amount of money spent as you spend it.

Date	Stock		Travel		Props		Rent	
MAY *14*	45	75	2	50			10	00
21	12	25	3	00	2	00	10	00
23	98	00	4	50				
28			2	50			10	00

JUNE *4*	4	50	2	50			10	00
11	120	00	2	50	1	00	10	00
17	38	50	3	00				
18			2	50			10	00
TOTAL JUNE *18*	319	00	23	00	3	00	60	00

In the sample above, as of June 18 you have spent:

$319.00 on your stock
23.00 on travel expenses
3.00 on props
60.00 on rent

A total of $405.00 on your flea market business
3. Label your second pad "income." It's a record of all the money your business takes in. Use two columns here.

Date	Stock Sold	
MAY *14*	98	00
21	104	75
28	140	00
JUNE *4*	118	50
11	122	25
18	168	00
TOTAL JUNE *18*	751	50

You now know that as of June 18 your flea market business took in $751.50, your gross income.
4. What is your net profit? For that, you need your third pad and four columns.

Date	Gross Income		Expenses		Net Profit	
JUNE 18	751	50	405	00	346	50

By subtracting expenses from gross income, you know that your net profit is $346.50.

If your net profit figure looks good to you, then keep on the way you've been going. But what if it doesn't? Begin right now to change it for the better (see Chapter 14, The Best Laid Plans).

To Keep

You have to decide how much of your net profit you want for yourself and how much you need to reinvest. If you work at a weekly flea market, you can figure out your average weekly net profit and decide on that basis, or you can let those profits build up for a month and then draw out one lump sum. But decide what percentage is yours for keeps. It may be ten, twenty-five, or fifty percent. Any more than fifty percent would starve the baby; any less than ten percent leaves the parent feeling hungry.

To Spend

Any part of your net profit you don't keep for yourself will go directly back into your business—to buy stock and to pay operating expenses, such as rent and travel. As we've said before, the more stock you buy, the more stock you will have to profit on. Do you want to build up your business fast and only then begin to take out your profit? Or do you need that money right now? Whether for economic reasons or because it's great for morale, if you need it, take it. Your business will grow more slowly, but it will grow.

For Tax

Your sales tax will vary, depending on which state and city your business is in. The best way to find out what it is and how to pay it is to call your local tax office and ask. Don't ask friends, other dealers, or anyone else. Get all your legal information from the correct legal source.

The sales tax is a hidden charge your customers pay. That is, you include it in your markup. Otherwise it will eat up too much of your profit. You must always be aware of that extra dollar or two. If a customer should ask, "What about tax?" you simply answer, "I pay the tax."

14

The Best Laid Plans

What's Wrong

A flea market dealer needs the answers to only two questions: Does my stock sell? Am I making money? It isn't hard to find honest answers to these questions.

When you pack up at the close of a show, stuff those cartons as compactly as you did when you first packed everything you were bringing. And try to get cartons that are about the same size. You know that you arrived at the market with twelve boxes. How many did you have when you left? Ten, eleven, eleven and a half, or maybe, happy day, five or six. Count those cartons. They tell the truth. Like Harry in Chapter 3, The Portable Shop, you could think of sale days in terms of how many cartons you sold. You might even keep a simple record.

Date	Name of Market	No. of Cartons Bought	No. of Cartons Left	No. of Cartons Sold
APRIL 3	Farmers Mart	12	10	2
APRIL 10	Super-Flea	12	8	4
APRIL 17	Farmers Mart	12	10½	1½

This type of notebook tells you at a glance:

1. Which markets are best for your business. If some markets cost you more in rent or traveling expenses, you'll know if they're worth it.
2. Which days are best for your business, which months.

Look hard at your third spiral pad, the one that shows your net profit. That figure is the truth. And you can't avoid it or ignore it, even if it's saying what you'd rather not hear. Listen to what those numbers are telling you. If you don't like the message, you *can* change it.

Creative Answers

If you decide to make changes, to look for new answers, make them creative ones. Does the problem lie with the market? You can't sell to nonexistent customers. Then the answer is simple. Move to a new market and keep on moving until your business improves.

The answer to a problem of stock is not quite so simple. If not enough people want whatever you are selling, you will have to make drastic changes. Walk around your market or visit another busy flea market when you aren't selling. Watch the browsers. What kinds of things are they picking up and stopping to look at? Watch the customers. What items are they buying? What is really going out of the dealers' hands and into the customers'? What exactly is money being paid out for? Whatever it is, that's the kind of item you want to have in your stock. And what it is can differ widely, depending on what part of the country you are in or even on whether you are selling in a city, suburb, or rural area. The only answer is to restock your business, slowly, gradually, using what you've learned from looking and watching. Put your new merchandise at the front of your tables and use the old to fill in empty spaces. As you gather together more of your new stock there will be less and less of the old displayed.

What can you do with the old?

Dom walked up to Janet one morning as she was unloading the back of her car.

"Here," he said, "I'll give you a hand. No help today?"

"No, I'm all alone. My son has a summer cold and I couldn't get a last-minute replacement."

"Don't worry, we're neighbors today and we can help out. Say, how about those four cartons at the back?"

"Oh, just leave them. It's some dumb stuff I bought when I first went into business. I don't know what to do with it, so it just sits in the back of the car, week after week."

"I can take care of that problem, the same way I took care of my mistakes. Have you got a blanket?"

"Sure, in the trunk."

"You spread it out on the ground, at the side of your table. Now unpack the junk and just lay it out on the blanket, right there on the ground. Now we'll turn this empty carton upside down and stack another on top, and another. The carton at eye level will have to be our sign. Got a wide pen?"

"No, I don't."

"I'll get mine. Hold on." In a few minutes he was back with a half-inch-wide black felt-tipped pen. Drawing large letters that covered the side of the box, he wrote:

IT'S ALL JUNK,
BUT IT'S ALL CHEAP!

"You bet it is," laughed Janet. "It's all junk, and I'm selling it cheap."

We watched as she did sell it, and in a few hours almost

all of it was gone. There's even a way to make "the worst" salable.

Do browsers rummage through your stock? Do the crowds stop? Do they look at and handle your merchandise? If they do, fine! But do they then put it all back, stop rummaging, and walk on? It doesn't take any heavy thinking to know that your problem is, in one word, "price." Be realistic. Why do most customers come and come again to the flea market to buy? It certainly isn't for the beautiful decor, the comfort, the heating or air conditioning, the sleek salespeople, the prestige label. It's for one reason only—to buy cheap, to find a bargain, that great buy they can't find in retail stores. If you don't give them any bargains, you're not playing the game by the rules. And in return most of your potential customers will pass you by! If you want to sell, you must give the customer what he wants. And he in turn will give you what you want—sales and profits. Price your merchandise low enough to sell. You will learn by experience what price is low enough to attract sales, but still high enough to ensure a profit.

Run with a Winner

Perhaps none of the above problems is yours. You flea market is crowded on every sale day. Your stock produces oh's and ah's from people as they stop and reach out. Your prices please them and the wrapping up and making change keep you busy all afternoon. In short, you have a winner. Run with it. Don't change a thing. Let all the other dealers watch you and mumble: "How do they do it?"

15

Pleasures and Bonuses

Cast of Characters

Janet	Susan	⎫
Dom	Alex	⎬ All Flea Market Dealers
Harry		⎭

Scene

A *neighborhood bar and restaurant, bright, well-lit, with large tables in back. Around one table sit our five characters. Dom and Harry are drinking beer, Susan and Alex drink coffee. Janet has a bottle of mineral water. Sale day is over. Their gear—stock, tables, etc.—is packed in their cars. Everyone is tired and looks a bit messy. Everyone looks happy.*

HARRY: That sure was one long day.

JANET: And a good thing too. I wouldn't have minded if it were twice as long.

DOM: Too bad all market days aren't like this one. Our only problem would be finding enough stuff for them to buy.

JANET: It must be something in the air that makes them all think "buy, buy" all on the same day. Every time this happens, I try to figure out why. What do each of the great sale days have in common? But I can't come up with an answer.

HARRY: I don't bother to think why. It's just luck. The more they want to buy, the better. Don't think so much or you'll kill your luck.

SUSAN: Half our stock is gone. Just think of all the work, replacing it in time for next week.

DOM: (*Laughing*) You may not need it all next week. Today was a bonus and they don't come that often.

HARRY: Don't discourage her, Dom. Listen, Susan, it's a good flea market. People shop every week. Sometimes they buy more, sometimes less. But you'll make out. We all do.

DOM: You left out the most important thing they have to know.

ALEX: What is the most important thing? I'd like to hear it.

JANET: Keep your prices reasonable. Or most of them anyway. Sometimes you can tack on a little extra, but don't get carried away. It's the day's total that counts, not any single sale.

HARRY: You sound like my high school Latin teacher, giving lectures. They're young, they're new in business. Let them learn from experience. Maybe they know better than us. Maybe they have new ideas to teach us.

SUSAN: Oh no, Harry, we could never teach you anything. I loved the answer you had for the woman in the rose print dress. The one who said that the framed silk with Teddy Roosevelt embroidered on it was too high. What was it you answered?

HARRY: I asked her the same question I ask every tightwad: "When was the last time you saw one just like it?" It stops them all, dead in their tracks. There is no answer. Even if they have seen another just like it last week, few people can think fast enough to shoot an answer back. They just stop and sigh, "You're right."

ALEX: Don't stop talking, Harry. Susan and I are learning more here than we did all day at the market. (*Everyone laughs. Janet applauds*)

JANET: You know, I always wanted to be my own boss. To work for myself, not for anyone else. But I couldn't manage to save enough money to open a shop. That's what I wanted, my own boutique. And now I've got it. All it took was $25 for my first day's expenses.

SUSAN: What did you sell that first day?

JANET: All the interesting bits and pieces I'd been gathering up for years: art deco jewelry originally from the dime store, scarves, antique clothes, square plastic handbags, a few beaded bags. I even had a pair of pure silk stockings, never worn, still in its box. It must have been pre-WorldWar II.

SUSAN: How could you sell those stockings? I would've kept them.

JANET: But they weren't my size. Besides, they were in such mint condition, I didn't have the nerve to unwrap them, much less wear them.

ALEX: I keep telling you, Susan, if you're in business you can't think in terms of keeping everything or keeping anything.

HARRY: You know, the flea market isn't like any other retail business.

ALEX: But the same rules still apply. Honest dealing, good reputation, good value, salable merchandise.

DOM: That's true. But the differences are important too. For one thing the flea market is the most democratic marketplace there is. No one asks your age, race, sex, or religion. And that's not just lip service to a nice idea. It's because no one there, whether dealer or customer, really gives a damn about who you are or what you are. As long as you give them what they want, at the price they want. Of course, it helps if you're honest and pleasant to deal with. That's all anyone asks for. And that's my lecture. After which I think I need another beer. Anyone else?

HARRY: Sure, I can always use another.

SUSAN: But nobody has said one word about how much fun it is. I just love it. The crowds. The noise. I love talking to people about old things. I get a good feeling every time I make a sale. I never knew I could do something like this.

ALEX: It's free enterprise, honey, at its most basic level. I'd like to keep it up until I retire. Then we could deal full time. Get a VW bus, pack in our stock, and travel to shows all up and down the coast. Summer in New England, spring in New York City, winter in Florida. Maybe even California.

DOM: Well, it's a good daydream. I hope you make it. But now I'd like to propose a very formal toast. (*Everyone laughs and stands up, glass or cup in hand*) To a fine, beautiful bonus day. May there be many more for all of us. (*Everyone drinks solemnly, then they all casually leave the bar*)

The End

Part II

The Customer

16

The Other Side of the Table

Your View

Making money is what flea markets are all about, and a great deal of that money has been made from your side of the table. You can choose to make that money directly or indirectly, but either way, that potential money is there waiting for you. That's one of the prizes you are hunting for through all the debris of times past.

Buying at flea markets carefully and deliberately, you can earn money indirectly by choosing bargains, so that the things you both need and want cost you a great deal less than if you bought them new in a retail store. At the same time, you will be buying quality—an ingredient disappearing fast from our retail markets. Shopping in flea markets, you quickly learn to forgo glossy newness in favor of lasting good quality and a lovely patina of age.

In search of such treasures you can follow a trail of fleas across and up and down North America, Europe, South America, and even the Far East. Every large city in the world has its open marketplace, where people stand and sell what they own and no longer want. Or what they've gathered together in hopes that others will want it. And you do want it. Not all of it, but just enough to surround yourself with the objects that remind you of the past and that give you an anchor of tradition.

Saving Money

You can be furnishing an entire home, or one room. Looking for one important piece, or all the details and accessories a working kitchen needs. Looking for an unusual gift for a friend or a present for yourself. Whatever it is, you have in mind a certain amount of money you know you can use for that purpose. Spending that money in a flea market, you will get twice as much in return for it or perhaps have a good deal of it left over—a very pleasant thought. In our present economy a feeling of having extra money, something left over, is possible only at flea markets, where good quality is recycled over and over again. You're saving money and enjoying it at the same time. The carnival spirit of the flea market, the suspense of never knowing just exactly what it is you might find on that particular day, are habit-forming attractions.

Earning Money

Almost anything you buy in a flea market can be resold by you later, if necessary. If you are careful in your buying, you will never have a problem of what to do with it all if you decide to redecorate or to move and travel light. It will always be worth at least what you paid and sometimes even more. The use you've gotten from your market finds in the meantime is a kind of bonus.

David had used his old electric toaster for three years. It was an early one, 1911 or 1912. The toast didn't pop up, as in modern electric toasters. The bread just sat there waiting to be turned around and then taken out of the toaster when done. But there was something about the design he liked. It brought back memories, and anyway it was his. The rest of the family had its own up-to-the-minute model.

The problem began with David's new apartment. It had a tiny kitchen. No room for two toasters, so the old one had to go. David decided to sell it to a flea market dealer. He had paid $5 for it originally. What could he get for it now after three years' use and care?

With the toaster under his arm David walked through the large flea market. A parking lot on weekdays, it was crowded with people every Sunday. He kept watching the tables as he walked, ignoring the dealers. Finally he found just the right table. It was covered with kitchen utensils of every generation of American life. Including early electrical appliances.

"I'd like to sell this toaster," said David, holding it out to the dealer. "It's in good condition, and it works. I used it this morning."

The dealer inspected it very carefully, turning it around, tugging on the wire. "All depends on the price." Shrugging, he handed the toaster back to David.

"Well, how much would you offer for it?"

"Oh, I never make an offer. You tell me what you want for it, and we can begin there."

David did some fast thinking. "How about $10?"

"How about $5?" the dealer quickly answered. "I pay rent and gas. Don't forget that."

"How about $8? It works. Don't forget that."

"Can you take $7?"

"OK, $7."

Leaving the flea market, David had a good feeling. He had made $2 profit on something he had used for three years. He certainly couldn't have done that with a brand new toaster.

YOUR PERSONAL BUYING SERVICE. YOURS FOR THE ASKING.

All the bazaars, rummages, house, yard sales
All the attics, basements, barns
All the mail order contacts with other dealers
And all the other sources dealers have that you don't

Dealer A
(on the phone)

Dealer B
(in an easychair)
doing mail order)

Dealer C (on the go)   You

"Maybe I ought to buy everything secondhand," thought David.

What Are You Buying?

A flea market is a free-for-all—no pattern, no design, unstructured. And that's the way to shop it. Keep an open mind. Look at everything. Think about possibilities. Do any of those objects mean anything to you? It's most important to be selective. You can't buy it all, you can't possibly use it all. Be careful. Buy what you need, buy whatever appeals to you, and buy it at a careful price.

What to Do with What You've Bought

Here are some ideas for new uses for old things:

Old tools: Paint them black and arrange a group of them on a white wall, for instant metal sculpture. Paint small tools in bright colors and hang on thin wire for an interesting mobile.

Broken old desks: Use the metal drawer pulls on new kitchen cabinets. Use a drawer, properly lined, for a cat's or dog's bed. The thin turned legs make towel racks for kitchen or bath. The section across the back with tiny cubbyholes can be hung above a table to store letters or paper. Painted white, it can be hung in the kitchen for spices. Or hang it over a dressing table for cosmetics, in the bathroom for soaps, etc. If the slant top has carving or a design in wood relief, refinish it and hang it on the wall, for instant wood sculpture. Or hang the top with its hinges against the wall and a supporting bracket underneath, giving you an extra shelf.

Old fabric: Patches mend antique quilts with authentic fabrics. Make your own quilt using bits of old silk prints. Use a lace tablecloth as a poncho. Rip the crochet trim from a pillowcase and use it to trim a blouse, slip, or nightgown. Take the appliqué work from linen napkins and decorate the neckline of a T-shirt. Cut out bits of old embroidery and trim jeans and denim jackets. Cut up a chenille bedspread and make a long wrap-around skirt. Or make chenille drapes for an art deco bedroom.

Carpeting: Cut out the bright, less worn sections and use them to make shoulder bags, tote bags, book covers. Trim a piece to the shape of a round table and slip it under a glass top for an interesting and unusual tabletop. Cut out one large flower or abstract design and frame it. It will look antique and expensive. Use it to cover small throw pillows for a couch.

Paper goods: Frame uncut paper dolls from old magazines and hang in a girl's bedroom. Frame a group of fashion prints from old magazines and hang them over a dressing table. Cover one small wall with blueprints and shellac it. Glue old restaurant menus on an entire kitchen wall. Glue interesting old bits of paper to the top of a coffee table and cover with a sheet of glass, hiding the damaged top of the coffee table at the same time. Frame and hang engraved business contracts over a desk.

Fancy tie racks: Hang in a bedroom to hold necklaces and scarves.

Buttons: Glue them onto earring backs, pin backs, or barrettes for interesting "antique" jewelry. Or string them on a chain and wear as a pendant.

Watches: The fancy backs and fronts of watches that will never work again make lovely jewelry. Taken apart, the inner workings can be used the same way as buttons.

Cigarette cases: Too small for modern cigarettes, you can use them to carry pocket change. The really fabulous cases make tiny evening bags, large enough for a door key and a little mad money.

Small clocks that don't work: Take out the clockworks and you have a picture frame.

Casseroles that have lost their lids: Use them as fancy containers for clay flower pots.

Pottery mugs with fine cracks: Fine for pencil or toothbrush holders.

Tall copper or brass pots that leak: Use as wastepaper baskets or containers for fireplace wood.

Iron lamp brackets: Paint them black and use for hanging plants.

Ornate muffin and tart tins: Paint them in bright colors and use for small cosmetics or desk supplies. Plain ones are fine for bits of hardware: nails, screws, etc.

Marble tops from wrecked furniture: Clean off and use as pastry boards or as sections of a kitchen counter.

You're sure to have ideas of your own. Do let us know of any that come your way. We're always on the lookout for more.

17

What Is a Bargain?

You Need It or Want It

The lure of the flea market is all rolled up into one word, "bargains." We all love a bargain. It's a great feeling when you know you've been clever enough to see what everyone else was blind to. You've beaten the system one more time. But what exactly is a bargain? What is it you look for?

1. You need it. It's something practical you're going to use. Hammer, pliers, and files for your workshop. You've gone to the hardware store, priced them, and turned pale. You've check the Sears catalogue and the discount store ads. You know what each item would cost you, new and clean. You've done your homework. Now shop the flea market, searching until you find just what you need. What's the condition of those tools? Are they rusty? Will you have to work on them to make them usable? Does their low price make the extra work worthwhile? If you come up with the right answer, buy them.

2. You want it. It's the most beautiful lace cloth you've ever seen. Every bit of it is handmade, lovingly made. You visualize it tacked down on an apricot-colored silk sheet and used as a bedspread. But how can you judge its value? Stores don't carry large pieces of handmade lace. Nobody makes it any more.

We already know that you really want it, that your hands itch to hold it and carry it home, so there is only one question left. Can you afford it? Only you can answer that question honestly. Will you have to forgo another pleasure to make this one possible? Think hard! If you can afford to buy it, it's a bargain. If you can afford it and don't buy it, you'll be sorry later.

It's Not Yet the Fashion

Stay away from the fashionable if you're looking for bargains. Fads are expensive. Suddenly everyone seems to be buying old wicker. The media pick up on it. Books are published about wicker. Facsimile editions of original wicker catalogues are advertised. The prices for good wicker furniture and accessories are continuing to climb. It will be years before those prices fall back to a commonsense level. For the time being, then, don't even think of buying wicker unless the question, "How much?" is irrelevant to you.

The secret is to buy what you like before there is a large demand for it, before it becomes the fashion and everyone is trying to buy it. It's a simple question of supply and demand. Fashion often has nothing to do with quality, beauty, or workmanship. You won't have to sacrifice any of these in the search for your bargains.

Trust Yourself

If you're not going to rely on fashion and the taste of others, and you certainly don't want to rely on price ("It costs more, so it must be better than the rest"), then what can you rely on? You must trust yourself. You already know what you like and what you want to own. You know which of the old and secondhand things you see in the flea market really appeal to you. Take that taste, your taste, and build on it. Keep your eyes open. Go to museums and historical restorations and learn what the real thing looks like. Go to antique shows and touch as much as you can. Find out what the real thing feels like. Learn what quality is and use that knowledge to find your bargains.

18

The Right Price

What Is It?

The right price is the price you want to pay. Dealers have only their own intuition and experience to guide them in pricing. The same holds true for you, the buyer. Just as you have to learn to read or to play tennis, you learn to buy: what you want, at the price you want to pay for it. If the price, after bargaining, is still more than you want to pay, you make a choice. You decide that your life will be just fine without that item, or you decide you can't live without it.

If you become a flea market regular, you will almost certainly become familiar with the type of secondhand merchandise that most interests you. You'll soon find yourself talking about it with the dealers who sell it. Once you establish yourself as a buyer who knows what he or she wants and knows the price he wants to pay, you will find many dealers ready to supply your wants at your price, if it is indeed a fair price.

Talk About It

Talking price can be just as interesting as anything else you talk about. It all depends on your tone of voice and the impression you leave with the dealers.

Allison's entire family was coming to help celebrate her housewarming. Three sons home from college, her sister's family, all five, and, of course, Allison's husband and her parents. That made a party of twelve. What could she serve? She decided that since they all liked seafood, it would be a stuffed striped bass, really huge, embellished with shrimps and mussels. The more she thought about it, the clearer the picture grew in her mind. There was only one thing missing —a platter long enough, wide enough, but not too wide, to hold that lovely steaming bass. So Allison got up early Sunday morning and drove out to the flea market, looking for a fish platter. And, of course, she found it.

Not only was the platter just the right size, but it had a painting of a bass down its entire three-foot length. The colors sparkled and the quality of the china background was firstrate. Allison stared straight at the platter, not even seeing the dealer. But he saw her and the look in her eye.

"It is beautiful, isn't it?" Dom asked in a soft voice. "It's the nicest fish set I've ever had."

"Set?" murmured Allison. "What set?"

"Why, the fish set you're looking at."

"I was looking at the platter. It's just what I need."

"Well, these twelve plates match. It's a set for eating fish, platter and twelve plates. Perfect condition and a good price."

"But I only want the platter. What are you asking for it?"

"I'm not asking anything for it. It goes with the set."

"All right," sighed Allison, "have it your way. What are you asking for the entire set?"

"It's $165," Dom replied, "and you won't find it anywhere for a price like that. It's the best buy today."

"But it's not a buy for me. I only . . ."

"I know. You only want the platter. But it would be a shame to break up the set. It's worth more when it's all together like that."

"Well, I guess I could find a use for the plates. But I really shouldn't have to pay full price for the set when I really only want a part of it. Couldn't you adjust your price in some way?"

"You mean, will I sell it to you for less than $165?"

"Yes, that's what I mean. I would pay $45 for the platter. That leaves $120 for the plates. And that's too much for twelve plates I don't even want."

"Mmmmm." Don was thinking out loud. "I did count on $10 per plate. Let's see, how about $8 apiece. That's knocking off $24. I must be crazy, but what the hell. A sale is a sale. Take it for $141."

Allison thought for a long minute. "If I'm paying $45 for something I want, I shouldn't have to pay more than double for what I don't want. And $45 doubled is $90, so how about $90 for the plates, plus the $45 for the platter, which is a total of $135 for the set. How does that sound to you?"

Dom threw up his hands. "I can't beat you, lady. It's a deal for $135 and you get some buy."

"Oh, thank you. I knew you wouldn't want me to break up the set."

That afternoon Allison walked into her house carrying a very heavy carton.

"Here, let me help," said George. "Say, I thought you were only going to look for a platter."

"I did look for a platter and I found a platter. But what's really wonderful is that I also found twelve plates to match it, a perfect set. I never expected such luck."

"What did all that cost?" wondered George.

Allison smiled. "The dealer was asking $165 for it, but by the time I finished talking the price was down to $135. I think it was a great bargain."

Allison did buy the fish set at a bargain price, but possibly $135 was Dom's bottom line all along.

Like Allison, you can always talk about the price with almost any flea market dealer. Be frank. Tell him what you want to pay, as pleasantly as you can. And he will be just as open with you. He will answer yes or no. It's that simple, and it makes your shopping much more interesting. The game of wits is the fun part.

Fantasies

When you are shopping the market, we hope you will leave your fantasies at home. Flea market fairytales all seem to be variations on what we call the Rembrandt-in-the-trash myth. That's just what it is: a myth. Despite all the stories you hear and read about, it is very, very rare (if not impossible) for anything of important value to be sold for $2 to $10. Dealers make it their business to know about their merchandise. You are only wasting your time and energy looking for that Tiffany glass lamp at the bottom of a barrel. The fantasy becomes a distraction. It gets in the way of the many good buys you can find at flea markets. Concentrate on those bargains realistically and you will find them.

Realities

Flea market dealers pay less rent than shopkeepers, have much lower expenses, and have more time to search out bargains. Most of them will pass on these good buys to you—the customer. After all, if the owners of antique shops can pay flea market prices and still sell at a profit, you're bound to find bargains there, too. That's reality, so take advantage of it. Go to the market often. The dealers' stocks change constantly. Look for what you want. Check out things you've never seen before that fascinate you. Don't be afraid to ask questions. The more you know about what's being offered for sale, the better shopper you become.

19

Your Own Collection

Everything Old Is Collectible

All those objects used in everyday life. whether in the recent or distant past, are collectibles. They include:

The things we once saw our mothers and fathers use, the things that perhaps we once used ourselves: utensils and implements, tools and artifacts
The clothing our grandparents wore
Their photos and the cameras that snapped those photos
Objects connected with your grandmother's kitchen and your grandfather's occupation
The magazines your grandparents read, the advertisements they saw, the premiums they were given, the calendars that hung on their walls.

You get a warm feeling when you hold some small piece

of the past in your hand. Well made, carefully used, lovingly kept, all these years. How pleasant it is to have our cake and eat it too, to enjoy the practical use of modern technology while creating our own collections of the old and leisurely. Your collection is made by you: chosen, arranged, and displayed by you. It's completely yours, and the admiration and respect of the people you show your collection to, those are also yours.

What to Collect

You really have to love it to collect it, whatever it is. Don't try to sit in an armchair and decide what it is you want to surround yourself with. Get out to all the flea markets you can reach. Visit all the antiques and collectibles shows you can. Keep your eyes open. Look at all the merchandise. The variety is astounding. Here is what you are looking for:

1. Something you recognize immediately. You feel a strong response as you look at it. Don't bother with anything that strikes you as merely pretty. If you look at it and then shrug, leave it there.

2. The things that are not manufactured any more because there is no longer a practical use for them. Here are a few:

> Hand-held fans
> Penholders
> Hatpins
> Shoebutton hooks
> Compacts for loose powder
> Straight razors
> Shaving mugs
> Blotters

3. Any type of old advertising or store display such as:

> Store counter displays
> Bar window signs
> Outdoor tin signs

Trade cards
Cigarette cards
Magazine ads

4. Old pieces of clothing in the styles popular before 1940.

5. All the memorabilia of the luxurious modes of travel that are no longer as elegant as they once were:

Ocean liners
First-class railways
Airliners (early cross-country passenger planes)
Long, elegant roadsters

6. Household items that have been replaced by electrical appliances:

Irons that were heated on stoves
Coffee grinders and roasters
Oil lamps
Iceboxes
Butter churns

7. The games and toys, the entertainments, like old phonographs and stereopticons, of past generations.

Does reading this list give you ideas? There are lots more, waiting for you to find them. The more obsolete your collectible is, the better. The more it was used originally, the better. The common and the ordinary are now the desirable and sought after.

Where to Find It

If your collectible is too easy to find there's no fun in it, no suspense, and that makes collecting dull. Thank heaven you have to go out and find it! When you get to a flea market, walk around. If you can't find the specific thing you're seeking, look for a dealer who handles similar merchandise and ask if he can find what you want. Tell him you are really interested in buying and will be back next week. It usually pays off.

Visit antique shows. Subscribe to the antique trade papers listed in Chapter 6, Where Does It All Come From? You can see, by reading the "Merchandise Wanted" sections of the classifieds, that many collectors advertise for their wants. It saves a lot of work to have dealers write to them about specific items in their category. How pleasant to be able to sit back and read a letter from a dealer, choose what you like, and mail off a check. Many collectors have hundreds of dealers, all over the country, looking for and searching out the things they want to buy and pay for. The dealer acts as your agent. You pay only for the things he actually buys for you. It means a bargain for you and a steady customer for him.

How to Display It

Now that you've begun to collect, what are you going to do with all that stuff? Don't let it overwhelm you. You can use that collection to make your home more attractive. Show it off. If it's china or glassware, build glass-enclosed shelving for it or invest in cabinets or bookcases with glass fronts. If you're collecting anything unbreakable—books or metal objects—open shelves are fine. Small collectibles—buttons, medals, and so on—can be displayed in special cases shaped like trays. Only one inch deep, they are lined with cotton or fabric and have glass or clear plastic covers. They can be grouped and hung on the wall, just as you'd hang a group of framed prints.

Interesting arrangements can be made with handbags and antique clothing or costume jewelry. Shallow cabinets can stand floor to ceiling, with your collection hanging from hooks. Glass doors protect anything fragile. There are collectors who have built special rooms, designed to hold and display their collections to best advantage. How far you want to go with this, how elaborate you want your display to be, is up to you. But there is no limit. Collecting can be a small, enjoyable part of your life, or it can grow and grow until everything else seems to take second place to that all-important collection.

Collectors' Clubs

No matter what you collect, there is somewhere in this country a club, a society, an organization devoting itself to making that object an even more popular collectible than it already is. If you want to enjoy your collecting as much as you possibly can, you'll join the clubs whose members are interested in the same things that appeal to you. If you collect postcards, there are many clubs open to you. They seem to be spread out over the entire country; some hold monthly meetings. There's even a Federation of Postcard Clubs. However, if you collect antique cookie cutters, there is only one club for you to join and one annual meeting for you to attend: the Antique Cookie Cutter Collectors' Convention.

There are hundreds of these clubs. The real fun of collecting is talking shop with others who collect the same things you do, swapping your duplicates for theirs, and acquiring the hard-to-find for your collection. Many collectors while traveling and searching for their own interests will also be on the lookout for a friend's collectible. Only another collector can appreciate the joys of a real find, the ultimate collectible, the one missing piece all collectors yearn for.

While there is no list of all these organizations that we know of, most of them are referred to in the pages of the antique trade papers we list in Chapter 6. Please don't hesitate. Write to the clubs that relate to your collection. You'll learn a great deal more about whatever you're collecting.

20

~~~~~~~~~~~

The Value of Collecting

Collecting for Resale

Professional collecting is an interesting and fun way to earn a substantial extra income. What's needed is a very real interest and love of collecting plus enough extra money—money you can afford to invest and allow to sit idle for a while until the ripe moment for selling the whole collection arrives.

1. Choose your collectible very carefully. Stay away from fads or any item that has been getting attention in the antique papers and magazines. Try to find an object that is interesting: to look at, to talk about, to think about. Does it have nostalgia value or teach us a bit of social history? One or two pieces may look vague or unimportant, but how about 50 or 100 or 10,000? Can you imagine the impact of a large grouping? Think before you begin to buy, because you will be buying a lot of whatever it is. Make your choice as specialized and

as old as it can possibly be. Not just Walt Disney characters, but a special one—Mickey Mouse, perhaps, and not just anything with Mickey on it, but only lamps shaped like Mickey or pull toys of Mickey. And made sure they date from the first phase of Mickey's popularity.

2. Resist the temptation to buy any item you find that fits into your category. Buy only those that are in good condition. Stay away from anything "restored" or pieced together—a top from here, a bottom from there, a new handle glued on. Keep it all authentic. Don't repair what you buy. Dust or wash it. Keep it clean. But don't polish and shine it too much. That patina of age is valuable. It took a long time to acquire. Be as selective as you can. A collection of duds is almost worthless.

3. Once you've made your choice, learn as much as you can about it. The more you know, the more complete you can make your collection. Talk to the dealers you buy from. Talk to other collectors. Read anything available on the subject. Look at and handle as much of it as you can. Become an expert and you'll increase your profit.

4. Don't be in a hurry. A collector needs patience. It takes time, lots of time, to find enough of your collectible. The more substantial your collection is, the more attention it will get when you are ready to sell. And attention means money.

5. Hold on to all of it. Keep buying more, and never sell bits and pieces of it no matter how tempting the money may be. Your collection will sell for a great deal more if it is a large one. It can never be too large or too complete.

When to Sell

An important part of the game is to pick the right moment to sell. The key word is *attention*. Gradually more and more attention will be paid to your collectible. Articles will appear in the "antique press." Large auction houses will begin to advertise it as an important part of their upcoming auctions. Art galleries will hold exhibits. Museum bulletins will refer to it. Dealers will suddenly begin to buy and sell it. Other collectors will form a club and advertise to buy it in "Antiques Wanted" columns. Keep your eyes open, and when you see that more and more attention is being paid to your collectible, then you know you can sell now for a good price. Or if you prefer, you can wait until public interest grows even more. The choice is up to you.

Where to Sell

Selling a large collection of anything takes time, just as it takes time to form that collection. Don't be in a hurry. You want to realize as much money from the sale as possible.

1. If you've been reading the antique trade papers as we've been telling you to throughout this book, you will have noticed ads for mail auctions. The ad usually describes a specific collection, large or small, and asks the readers to mail their offers to buy the collection to the advertiser. There is always a time limit: "Will accept bids up to two weeks after publication date." Read these ads and follow their pattern. Be honest about describing or listing your collection. And don't advertise unless you really are ready to sell. A reputation for playing games is not what you want. Honest and frank dealing will put more money in your pocket in the long run. If the highest bid is a price that means a good profit to you over the amount the collection has cost you, accept it. Make the sale. You now have your investment back, and you can begin again with another collectible. Most important of all, you also have your cash profit.

2. Type up a list and a description of your collection. Visit the antique and art galleries in your nearest large city. Find out if any of them are interested in your collection. They might want to buy it outright or sell it for you on consignment. Find out the exact terms of sale. Get it all down in writing, each one of you getting a copy of a signed contract. Better to be cautious than sorry.

3. Contact the large auction galleries that advertise specialized auctions. An auction of nothing but cut glass will realize higher prices for each piece of glass than if it were sold at a general auction. Collectors will travel to buy if they can choose from a large selection. You will realize more profit if your collection is sold at an auction of just that one category. Again it's important to have a signed contract, with all the dollar details spelled out. What is the gallery's commission? When do you get your money? Who is responsible for loss or damage?

How Much Profit

How much money you make on your collection is up to you. It depends on how clever you are in your original choice of what to collect, on how careful you are in your buying, on when you decide to sell. Remember that all this takes time and patience. If you need to earn this money right now or on a regular basis, find another way. You should be using only money you can afford to play with.

And it is play—play with potential profit. As any flea market fan—dealer or customer—will be happy to tell you.

Index